T2-CSE-085

At Issue

Child Athletes

Other Books in the At Issue Series:

At Issue

Child Athletes

Christine Watkins, Book Editor

GREENHAVEN PRESS

An imprint of Thomson Gale, a part of The Thomson Corporation

Detroit • New York • San Francisco • New Haven, Conn. • Waterville, Maine • London

Christine Nasso, *Publisher*
Elizabeth Des Chenes, *Managing Editor*

© 2008 The Gale Group.

Star logo is a trademark and Gale and Greenhaven Press are registered trademarks used herein under license.

For more information, contact:
Greenhaven Press
27500 Drake Rd.
Farmington Hills, MI 48331-3535
Or you can visit our Internet site at http://www.gale.com

LIBRARY OF CONGRESS CATALOGING-IN-PUBLICATION DATA

Child athletes / Christine Watkins, book editor.
    p. cm. -- (At issue)
  Includes bibliographical references and index.
  ISBN-13: 978-0-7377-3785-1 (hardcover)
  ISBN-13: 978-0-7377-3786-8 (pbk.)
  1. Sports for children. 2. Sports for children--Psychological aspects. 3. Sports for children--Social aspects. 4. Athletes. I. Watkins, Christine, 1951-
  GV709.2.C45 2008
  796.083--dc22
                                       2007020529

ISBN-10: 0-7377-3785-9 (hardcover)
ISBN-10: 0-7377-3786-7 (pbk.)

Printed in the United States of America
10 9 8 7 6 5 4 3 2 1

Contents

Introduction

During a Sunday pee-wee football game at Burholme Park in Philadelphia, Wayne Derkotch pulled a loaded gun on his child's coach because Derkotch felt his child was not getting enough playing time. A dentist in Albuquerque, Minnesota sharpened the face mask of his son's football helmet in order to slash opposing players. During a youth baseball game, a Pennsylvania policeman gave a pitcher two dollars to hit a ten-year-old batter with a fastball. Parents like these are ruining what used to be a good thing. Studies have shown that participation in sports offers important benefits for children such as physical fitness and emotional well-being, as well as valuable life lessons about teamwork, commitment, and sportsmanship; however, many experts believe that parents have become overzealous about sports and are undermining those benefits. "Youth sports have become about more than kids having fun," said Steve Marshall, an assistant professor of epidemiology and orthopedics at the Injury Prevention Research Center at the University of North Carolina in Chapel Hill. "Frankly, it's beginning to get out of control."

Of course there are parents who play a positive role in their children's athletic experience, driving to practices and games, being supportive whether they win or lose, trying to be fair to all players and coaches, and letting the kids just have fun. But for many other parents, it is all about winning. "Instead of unconditional love, too many kids are getting pressure—pressure to win, pressure to excel, pressure to make the all-star team, pressure to make Mom and Dad proud," wrote Joel Fish, author of *101 Ways to Be a Terrific Sports Parent*. Perhaps lured by dreams of college scholarships and lucrative professional athletic contracts for their child, parents are investing thousands of dollars on equipment, private trainers, sports camps, and tournaments. As a result, youngsters are feeling overwhelming pressure to be the best at their sport, and child psychologists are seeing increased rates of depression and anxiety disorders. Children need to be cared for as children; instead, they are being cared for as athletes. As Dan Potts, owner of the Advanced Athlete training facility in Seattle, illustrates, "I had a parent talking to me about her eleven-year-old son the other day. And she said, 'Well, what about his career?' I told her, 'He's eleven! He doesn't have a career!'"

Aside from the adverse psychological effects, pushing too hard too young can result in adverse physical effects as well. Children are especially vulnerable to injury because they are still growing. According to the American Academy of Orthopedic Surgeons, every year 3.5 million kids under the age of fourteen need medical care for sports injuries. Once virtually unseen in young athletes, overuse injuries such as "little league elbow" (damage to the growth cartilage in the elbow joint) and patellar pain syndrome (an alignment problem in the knee) have become widespread—so widespread, in fact, that clinics specifically for pediatric sports medicine have opened. And to make matters worse, often kids will not admit that they feel sore and will continue to play in spite of having an injury. As an example, seventeen-year-old Angel Bush blew out her knee while playing soccer. Despite the pain, she continued to run on it for three months "because my mom and my coaches told me to." After an MRI revealed the seriousness of her injury, her doctor recommended immediate surgery.

Another dangerous repercussion of the "winner-take-all" mentality of today's youth sports is the growing number of children who turn to steroids to give them that all-important edge over the competition. Despite the health risks involved—such as liver disease, heart arrhythmia, abnormal blood clotting, even death—more than one million U.S. high school students are estimated to have tried the body-altering drugs; up to 5 percent of high school girls and 7 percent of middle-schoolers admitted trying them at least once. At a congressional hearing in 2005, athletic and medical specialists agreed that their number one concern was steroid use by young athletes. "Most parents would be shocked to learn, as I was, that teenagers use veterinary-grade anabolic steroids from Mexico—drugs made for horses, cattle, and pigs," said Texas state representative Phil King. What is most frightening is that these student athletes acknowledge that steroid use is a form of cheating and understand the health risks, yet still continue to use the drugs because of the physical advantage they provide. Virginia congressman Tom Davis noted, "I can only wonder how we've arrived at a place where the drive to win is more important to some than not cheating, or not risking permanent harm to your health."

Parents today take sports and winning far too seriously. "In many cases, the biggest challenges are putting the games into perspective and finding balance—between sports and school, playing hard and playing dirty, winning and losing," Kelly Wallace noted in the *CNN.com* news article, "The Pressures of Kids' Sports: Competition Can Tax Time, Patience and Integrity." For children to gain the many benefits available from participating in sports, parents need to redirect their focus back to old-fashioned fun and fair play. This topic and many others are further discussed in *At Issue: Child Athletes*.

1

Playing Sports Benefits Children

Jordan D. Metzl and Carol Shookhoff

Jordan D. Metzl, medical director of the Sports Medicine Institute for Young Athletes, is a medical contributor to CBS News and has published widely in the field of sports medicine. Carol Shookhoff writes on educational issues and is the mother of a young athlete.

Playing sports is not only fun for children, but also offers benefits that affect other aspects of their lives. For example, when young people participate in sports, they have an opportunity to learn self-discipline, consideration of others, and how to handle disappointments. Also, the stress relief and physical fitness that result from playing sports help combat childhood depression and obesity, which has risen to epidemic proportions nationwide. Furthermore, researchers have found that girls who play sports reap particular benefits, such as a healthy body image, increased self-esteem, and a reduced risk of chronic disease. Girl athletes also are less likely to begin smoking or become pregnant as teenagers. Playing sports offers many physical, emotional, and social rewards that are not generally accorded to nonathletes.

When kids are asked why they play sports, here's what they say:

- To have fun

- To improve their skills

- To learn new skills

- To be with their friends

- To make new friends

- To succeed or win

- To become physically fit

Kids usually get the benefits they seek from sports and more. Kids need attention and respect (in that order), but they have few ways to get them. What is unique about sports is that they offer kids an arena where they can earn attention and respect by exerting their natural abilities. Kids are good at sports because sports are essentially about speed, strength, coordination, vision, creativity, and responsiveness—the necessary physical attributes are the attributes of youth.

Given that athletics involves all aspects of the human being, it is not surprising that participants benefit in all of the areas they mention. According to researchers at the Institute for the Study of Youth Sports at Michigan State University, kids who participate in organized sports do better in school, have better interpersonal skills, are more team oriented, and are generally healthier.

Participation in sports provides opportunities for leadership and socialization, as well as the development of skills for handling success and failure.

Moreover, when playing games, children learn how rules work. They see how groups need rules to keep order, that the individual must accept the rules for the good of the group, that rules entail a consideration of the rights of others. They also learn about competition, but within a restricted and safe system where the consequences of losing are minimized.

Benefits for girls have been of particular interest to researchers. The President's Council on Physical Fitness and Sports reports many developmental benefits of participating in youth sports for girls, including increased self-esteem and self-confidence, healthier body image, significant experiences of competency and success, as well as reduced risk of chronic disease. Furthermore, female athletes "do better academically and have lower school dropout rates than their nonathletic counterparts."

The Women's Sports Foundation lists many ways that sports specifically benefit female athletes. These include their being less likely to become pregnant as teenagers, less likely to begin smoking, more likely to quit smoking, more likely to do well in science, and more likely to graduate from high school and college than female nonathletes. Female athletes also take greater pride in their physical and social selves than their sedentary peers; they are more active physically as they age; they suffer less depression. There is also some evidence that recreational physical activity decreases a woman's chances of developing breast cancer and helps prevent osteoporosis.

I am convinced that sports offer a unique arena in which children can successfully exert their talents. The arena is unique for two reasons. First, sports engage the child as a complete human being: all facets—not just physical, but also social, cognitive, and psychological—are engaged harmoniously in striving toward peak fulfillment. Second, sports involve youths working in an ongoing community composed of their peers as well as their peers' families. Sports, that is, offer children an exhilarating, satisfying, rewarding way to participate in a larger world not generally accessible to nonathletes.

Physical Benefits

Fitness. Kids who play sports develop general physical fitness in a way that's fun, and they establish lifelong habits for good health. This is particularly important at a time when obesity in the United States has reached epidemic proportions: the incidence of obesity has increased by more than 50 percent among America's children and teens since 1976 and continues to grow at a staggering rate!

Stress relief. Sports allow kids to clear their minds of academic and social pressures, to literally run off the tension that's accumulated in their muscles. In the words of one patient, "If you play really hard, you feel better because playing takes your mind off things that bother you, and afterwards you can concentrate better." Most doctors recognize the positive mental effect of physical exertion, even though we're not sure exactly why this is so. I know that my ability to study in college and medical school was greatly enhanced when I ran during the day, and I'm not the only athlete to find this true. Many athletes get better grades in-season (theories posit the discipline and the need to manage time, along with an increased ability to concentrate). During exams, Duke University opens its gyms twenty-four hours a day to provide stress relief for its students.

Mastery. Sports give kids a satisfying, enjoyable way to develop their own talents: through personal effort they get good at something they're interested in. Doing something well makes them feel good about themselves, but equally important, it teaches them about the process of how to improve and work more effectively. Learning a skill—to dribble left-handed, say, or to execute an effective second serve—entails a recognition that practice is essential and that improvement is incremental. The process of repetition teaches the athlete how to master a move and also how to experiment with different approaches to improve a skill. The feedback in sports is usually immediate and visible—does the ball go into the basket?—so that the athlete can change or repeat what she's doing and figure out how to get better. Not only that, the whole process of seeing practice lead to improvement gives kids a feeling of control, a feeling all too rare in their lives.

Healthy habits. Because sports increase an awareness of one's body and how it responds to different stimuli and circumstances, sports help prevent drug and alcohol abuse. Most athletes value what their bodies can do and want to maintain those abilities. Being an athlete also gives kids an acceptable reason for telling their friends no to drugs, booze, and other high-risk, unhealthy behaviors. (Of course, not all athletes avoid drugs and alcohol.)

Personal Benefits

Valuing preparation. Sports help kids learn to distinguish between effort and ability. Sports increase self-discipline and the awareness of the value of preparation because kids can see the difference in their performance.

Competitive athletes learn the importance of effort, being prepared (mentally and physically), and enlightened risk-taking. They see that raw physical talent is not always sufficient to win the game, but that preparation is essential. This includes mental preparation (staying focused) and physical fitness as well as practicing the plays with their teammates in team sports. They learn to evaluate risk versus reward. Another invaluable lesson is discovering that mistakes are part of learning; they signal that a particular approach is unsuccessful and you must try another. Kids also learn to deal productively with criticism as part of improvement and preparation.

Resilience. Sports provide an unparalleled model for dealing with disappointment and misfortune. Young athletes learn to handle adversity, whether it's picking themselves up after losing a big game or not getting as many minutes as they wanted. They find ways to deal with losing and go on, because there's another big game next week or next year. They figure out what to do to get what they want for themselves. They put in extra time on fitness or work on specific weaknesses in their game (long-ball trapping, hitting to the opposite field, looking the ball into their hands). . . .

Long-term thinking. Athletes learn the fundamental lesson of sacrificing immediate gratification for long-term gain. This is the basis for personal success as well as for civilization in general, and no lesson can be more valuable.

Social Benefits

Sports are a social activity. Team sports are obviously done with other people, but even individual sports are often done as a team (tennis, golf, track). All sports, however, are intended to be performed in front of others, and the social ramifications are many. Here are some of them.

Relationships with other kids. Athletes develop relationships with their teammates. For boys, sports are a primary, and unfortunately sometimes the sole, way of socializing with others. In many schools and communities, nonathletic males find it difficult to develop a social network at all. For girls, who according to the feminist theorist Carol Gilligan tend to define themselves through their relationships rather than their achievements, sports offer yet another way to make friends and create an alternate peer group. According to Mike Nerney, a consultant in substance abuse prevention and education, multiple peer groups are always a good idea for teens, who have an intense need for inclusion and belonging, but who can also be volatile, cruel to each other, and foment destructive behavior as a group. Having a refuge when relations go wrong with one group can alleviate a great deal of stress and offer an alternative for kids who feel uncomfortable or frightened by peers who engage in high-risk activities.

Teamwork. On a team, kids learn about cooperation, camaraderie, give-and-take. They learn that while their natural position might be wide receiver, the team needs a cornerback, so they sacrifice their personal desires and play defense. They learn that you don't have to like someone in order to work together toward a common goal. They also discover that you can work for people you don't respect and still be productive, improve your skills, and have fun. A team is a natural environment in which to learn responsibility to others you can't stay out carousing the night before a game; sometimes you need to pass up a party in order to show up and play well.

Kids learn these lessons from their teammates and, most important, a coach who encourages the good of the team over the needs of an individual player. This attitude is sometimes rare in today's sports climate, where what's glorified is to "be the man." I think the earlier the message is instilled about the good of the larger whole, the better for kids in the long run.

Diversity. Organized sports sponsored by clubs or youth leagues not affiliated with schools offer players an opportunity to meet a variety of kids from different backgrounds. Students from public, private, and parochial schools come together in a common enterprise, crossing socioeconomic and ethnic lines, so that over time all players broaden their sense of how other people live. The genuinely multicultural environment is of tremendous importance in our polarized society. Kids play on the same team, wear the same uniform, share the same objectives and experiences. Sports are a great equalizer: rich or poor, black, brown, or white, are irrelevant. What counts is talent and heart.

Relationships with adults. When coaches, parents, and kids see each other at practice and games week after week, year after year, the adults learn to admire and praise the kids' prowess and progress, even when kids are as young as third graders. This kind of attention helps youngsters learn to balance their own evaluation of their improving skills with the appraisal of others who are not blood relatives; they also begin the lifelong process of figuring out whom to listen to when they hear conflicting advice or assessments. In addition, for young athletes of all ages, attention from interested adults is not only flattering but also helps them overcome shyness and develop poise when talking to relative strangers in social situations. The ability to feel comfortable in a variety of social circumstances will be progressively more valuable in a world of multiple cultures and decreasing numbers of supportive communities. . . .

Participating in a community. Sports foster a sense of community: they give both participants and spectators the experience of belonging to something larger than themselves, the need for which seems to be hard-wired into the human brain. This is why kids love playing for their schools, why high school football games in small cities can draw tens of thousands of spectators week after week, and why adults identify with their college teams years after they have graduated. Playing for an institution or a community gives kids a chance to feel that they are making a genuine contribution to a larger group. . . .

When playing for school or club teams, young athletes are afforded the opportunity to see how grownups and children treat one another and how this treatment has long-term consequences. They can see which adults care about kids, are willing to do their fair share and more, and take a stand for what they believe in. They see which parents are cooperative—pitching in to help with snacks, driving their kids' teammates to games, serving as team treasurer, volunteering to line the fields on cold, rainy mornings. They hear parents screaming at the officials and recognize which ones know the rules and which don't. They see who supports their own children and others, who bullies their children or the officials. They see parents who teach their children to assume they are always right, are better than the other players, and that someone else, anyone else, is always at fault if things go wrong. They also see how the kids in these families emulate or reject their parents' behavior. They think about how they will treat their own children and how they will behave with their friends as members of groups.

One hockey father says, "Part of the benefit of sports is that children observe its complex social dynamic among coaches, parents, players, and officials. There's a wide range of ethics, such as the attitude toward authority. Do you try to abide by the spirit of the rules, get away with what you can, accept what an official says, or do you argue and yell at him, or complain about it? Another major element they encounter is the difference between teammates who are good at communicating and sharing versus those who are out to get what they can for themselves. This is a dichotomy adults face throughout life. Kids involved in sports have to consciously or subconsciously figure out where they fit into those various spectrums."

Participating for years on the same team not only improves the play, because the players learn each other's strengths and weaknesses and where they'll be on the field or court, but it gives kids a wider view of the world and the people in it.

2

Playing Sports Can Harm Children

Deborah Mitchell

Deborah Mitchell is a freelance writer who specializes in health and earth-friendly issues.

At younger and younger ages, child athletes are experiencing intense training schedules, pressure to be the best at their sport, and painful, often serious injuries. Because children have not finished growing and their coordination and motor skills have not fully developed, they are exceptionally susceptible to injuries such as "little league elbow," Achilles tendonitis, and shin splints. Moreover, because of increasing pressure to win, these young athletes will often continue to play despite injury or pain, which can result in permanent damage. Even cheerleading has become a dangerous sport; a study by the University of North Carolina at Chapel Hill found that between 1982 and 2004, competitive cheerleading led to more catastrophic injuries than every other sport combined, including men's football. Unfortunately, children's sports as a whole have become so competitive that unless certain safety guidelines are met, young athletes are at risk for physical and emotional harm.

Eleven-year-old Brandon Sanford, a sixth-grader in North Texas, began taking tae kwon do at age 7. He won a bronze medal in tae kwon do poomse (forms) at the 2005 US Junior Olympics in San Antonio. Brandon trains 2 to 3 hours per day in the gym, four days each week and spends an additional day conditioning at the track.

Alicia Goodwin is a junior at Spring Creek Academy, a private school where Olympic hopefuls squeeze a day's worth of learning into three hours. Shorter school days allow Alicia to train 36 hours every week for the Junior Olympic Nationals. The young gymnast, who started the sport at age 9, has won several state and regional championships as well as the Western National Championship.

More young children than ever are pushing their physical and emotional limits in pursuit of athletic excellence, competing more fiercely and at younger ages. In their desire to be No. 1, they are undereating, overtraining and using illegal supplements and steroids. Competition is not just proverbially tough; it is becoming an all-consuming endeavor, which prompts the question, "How much is too much for our youngsters?"

"The No. 1 purpose of sports is to enrich the life of the child," says Dr. Jason Terk, a pediatrician with Cook Children's Physician network. "If the sport is doing this, then that's great. If it's not, or if it's causing great injury, then parents should keep kids out of the sport."

[C]hildren can suffer from long-term pain, arthritis and, on rare occasions, bone malformations.

According to the U.S. Consumer Product Safety Commission, more than 3.5 million children under the age of 14 suffer sports-related injuries each year in the United States. Young athletes are particularly susceptible to injury for several reasons: their coordination and motor skills are still developing, and their bones have not finished growing and hardening. And because children mature at different rates, there is the additional problem of inequity in height and weight among the same age groups.

Terk has seen the effects of competition taken to extremes. Sometimes, when a young athlete is hurt, a coach will discourage the child from seeking medical care and will ask him to first see the trainer about the injury. "The best decisions are not always made on behalf of the child," notes Terk.

Other times, it is the child who doesn't want to seek medical attention since it might mean lost opportunities, such as scholarships or tournament wins. Terk remembers one adolescent girl who fell during a soccer match, injuring the scaphoid bone in her wrist. "If you fracture that bone, it has a nasty habit of causing permanent problems," Terk says. "Sometimes surgery is required to put it back together." Because she wanted to continue playing soccer, the adolescent did not seek medical attention for a month, and, by that time, her wrist required surgery.

Practice, Practice, Practice

"With the increase in select sports, we are seeing more stress, overuse injuries," says Dr. David Gray, director of Orthopedics at Cook Children's Medical Center.

Fifteen years ago [1991], children used to play a different sport every season. Now, a young child may show interest or talent in one sport and want to specialize, which means playing the same sport all year. This makes kids susceptible to repetitive-use injuries; because the same set of muscles is used and the same set of motions are made repeatedly.

A common overuse injury is "little league elbow"—damage to the elbow joint resulting from the repetitive motions in pitching and hitting. This injury can take months to heal and sometimes may even require surgery. Terk cautions that wrestling and football are also culprits in repetitive-use injuries. Kids participating in these sports are particularly susceptible to back injuries, which may carry over into adulthood if the injury is not treated. But, oftentimes, treatment requires rest, and that's the last thing a youth athlete wants to hear when he has a big game coming up.

Children are also uniquely susceptible to "growth site injuries." Until the ages of 18 to 21, their bones are still developing and strengthening. Vulnerable growth sites—for example, the areas at the ends of longer leg bones—are the weakest part of the skeleton and the most prone to injury, especially from repetitive use. Children can suffer runner's knee, jumper's knee, Achilles tendonitis and shin splints. If the injuries are not diagnosed accurately, or treated properly, children can suffer from long-term pain, arthritis and, on rare occasions, bone malformations.

Overtraining not only puts a strain on growing bodies, it worries competitors.

Does Brandon Sanford's mom worry that he is pushing himself too hard? "No, but I do worry about him competing against kids that push themselves harder than he does," discloses Holly. "I worry about the chance of injury during sparring against kids who are more developed or have more experience."

[T]he risk of injury is always a concern. . . .

This year [2006], Brandon will be competing for the first time in tournaments that allow kicks to the head. His mom worries about the kicks coming from kids who train twice as much as her son. "Brandon wears the proper protection," Holly says, "and we have upgraded his gear, but it still doesn't make me worry free."

Pushing Through the Pain

Gymnastics is also one of the leading sports for injuries among children, and the risk increases with the level of competition. "I've been injured a lot—my elbows, hamstrings, back, and knees," Alicia says. She is currently being treated for a hamstring injury by a chiropractor, but that doesn't slow her down much. "The injuries last, but then you push through it."

Alicia's sense of competition is a strong internal force, says her mother, Julie. "Alicia pushes herself to be the best and at the top of whatever she is involved in." Her daughter maintains a 3.9 GPA in spite of her rigorous schedule. "We have never wished Alicia did not push herself because that is her personality. We as her family are there to enable her to fulfill her dreams and goals by supporting and encouraging her."

But the risk of injury is always a concern, and her mother notes that Alicia has had her share. "Yes, we are always concerned about injuries. You have to have confidence in the coaches to know that your daughter is ready to perform the big skills."

For elite gymnasts, there are added anxieties. Nature's call for puberty can be the end of a gymnastics career. Growth of breasts and hips can change a young woman's center of gravity, making moves that used to be easy, awkward. Some young women try to slow the onset of puberty and hold on to their prepubescent shape by keeping their weight down, which affects their health and development. Women's gymnastic champions have dropped in average age and weight over the years. This added pressure has produced eating disorders in some young gymnasts, resulting in additional developmental, psychological and long-term health issues. Famous Olympians Kathy Johnson and Nadia Comaneci have talked openly about their struggles with eating disorders and about the potentially harmful mentality of women's gymnastics. . . .

The Most Dangerous Sport

Remember when cheerleading was not a sport, but an activity to show your support for a favorite team? Not any longer. Competitive cheerleading is serious business and is now considered by many to be the most dangerous sport—even more dangerous than men's football. One study by the University of North Carolina at Chapel Hill found that competitive cheer leading had more catastrophic injuries between 1982 and 2004 than every other sport combined.

The pressure to perform and to be No. 1 causes performance anxiety in many of the young athletes.

The American Academy of Pediatrics recently released a report (January 2006) confirming cheerleading as "an important source of injury to girls." Injuries range from strains, sprains, head and neck injuries to paralysis and even death. As the sport grows increasingly competitive, young athletes are required to perform riskier stunts and gymnastic maneuvers. More girls than ever are suffering physical injuries and emotional distress from the pressure.

When Jennifer [name has been changed], a North Texas-area youth, began competitive cheerleading several years ago, she and her mother had to sign a contract with the gym stating that the program was not a recreational program, but a competitive one. "The gym definitely wants their teams to be No. 1," Jennifer's mother, Vicki, says. "The sport is on the extreme side, and it is very competitive."

The pressure to perform and to be No. 1 causes performance anxiety in many of the young athletes. Jennifer's sister, Renee [name has been changed], was a cheerleader at one time, as well. The intense demands of competition and of upholding her role on the team, however, caused her to "freeze up" in her tumbling routines—an anxiety that was felt by other girls at the gym.

"We have had girls sick and vomiting before a competition but still go out and compete so that they don't let the team down," says Vicki. She realized the high-pressure environment was not good for Renee and pulled her from the program, but the young girl faces self-esteem issues from the experience that she is still working to overcome.

In the quest to be the best, young athletes devote a large part of their week to training. During competition season, Jennifer practices almost every day of the week. Sometimes, the young athlete is so exhausted she comes home crying, says her mother. But high expectations and commitment to the rest of the team keep her going. Weekend competitions require even more time, as well as sacrifice from the rest of the family. Cheering events can consume the entire weekend between travel, competing and award ceremonies.

While Jennifer and Renee have struggled under the pressure and the time commitment, both are lucky. Neither has sustained physical injuries in this sport that has gained a reputation as the most dangerous sport for women. "Unfortunately," says their mother, "there are many girls at the gym that are on the injured list." . . .

Olympic Sports

Though coaches recruit very young children to become elite athletes, some physicians say that the low odds of winning an Olympic medal are not worth the risks to children's physical and emotional well-being. Concerns over the physical risks, as well as the emotional rigors of elite competition, led to the establishment of minimum-age guidelines. The International Olympic Committee requires that a competitor must turn 14 years old by the end of the Olympic year. Some sports, such as gymnastics require a minimum age of 16.

Bones Are at Risk

Dr. David Gray, director of Orthopedics at Cook Children's Medical Center notes that an increasing number of overuse injuries involve the growth plates of bones, which can lead to fractures. In rare instances, the growth plate can stop growing. "If pain persists directly over a boney area, especially at the end of a long bone—wrist, elbow or shoulder—that does not improve with a week of rest," Gray advises, "then there may be a stress, overuse inflammatory process involving the bone and growth plate that requires rest or significant modification in activities."

Gray offers these guidelines for parents and coaches:

- An important part of prevention is a diligent stretching program before and after activities.

- Vary activities from one practice to another to allow periods of rest from repetitive motion activity.

- Activities that require a lot of hyperextension of the lower spine should include stretching exercises of the upper and lower extremities, as well a core trunk strengthening program such as Pilates or yoga.

- Parents should realize that children and adolescents require rest and their bodies need time to recover from strenuous activities.

Introducing as much variation as possible in activities minimizes these stress, overuse injuries, which can put a young athlete out of a sport for 3 to 6 months.

3

Girls Benefit from Playing Sports

Julie Clancy Grady

Julie Clancy Grady is the news editor of Trinity Magazine, *the alumnae magazine of Trinity College in Washington, DC. She has four daughters who actively participate in sports.*

Ever since 1972, when it became law for schools to give girls the same opportunities as boys to play sports (Title IX), more and more young women are thriving physically, emotionally, and mentally as a result. Studies have shown that girls who participate in athletics have a lower risk for obesity and reproductive problems, have higher self-esteem, a better body image, and more academic success than nonathletic girls. As an added benefit, girls who play sports are less likely to smoke or experiment with drugs, alcohol, and sexual intercourse. Many young women will not develop the confidence or ability to become involved in sports in later years if they do not start participating at an early age; therefore, having access to physical education classes in grade school is crucial. The life lessons that can be learned from playing sports are so valuable that everything possible should be done to get and keep girls involved in athletics.

Finally, it seems, women's sports are catching up. Turn on ESPN [TV sports channel] and you'll likely see [tennis player] Serena Williams ace a serve or grab your local newspaper to read highlights of a girls soccer game. Look even harder and you'll find stories on women's hockey teams in Boston or women's wrestling at the University of Minnesota. It's only taken 30 years since Title IX [the federal educational amendment that bans sex discrimination] was enacted in 1972, and though there is still progress to be made, the payoffs are finally starting to appear.

And those rewards are more than a TV sound bite or color photo and feature story. From the professional paid athletes down to the first-graders in physical education class, women's sports offer a multitude of benefits that impact young girls throughout their entire life. Get a girl interested in sports, the experts say, and chances are you'll get a girl who exudes confidence, is physically healthy and is a success story waiting to happen.

Sports Have Many Benefits

According to the Women's Sports Foundation, a New York-based advocacy group for women's athletics, girls who are active in athletics have higher self-esteem, more confidence, better body image, higher achievement test scores, less depression, improved mental health, more academic success and greater lifetime earning potential. In addition, girls who play sports are also more likely to turn away from risky behavior, such as smoking, experimenting with drugs and alcohol, and sexual intercourse.

Jeanne A. Blakeslee, dean of students at St. Paul's School for Girls in Brooklandville, Md., can attest to these benefits first hand. With some 430 students in grades 5-12 and sports being an active part of student life, Blakeslee sees the advantages on a daily basis.

"Sports drives our lives," she said. "Sports are critical to girls because they are active and directive, and they have a lot of adults inserted into their lives that are not their parents and teachers, which is always good."

Blakeslee reports that from sports, girls learn teamwork. "They learn to be a star, gracefully or not. They learn how to support others and to make quick decisions. They are taken seriously because society acknowledges the importance of sports."

Physical Education: The Starting Point

For most girls, exposure to sports begins with physical education (PE) in grade school. Although many girls have the opportunity to play in organized sports leagues, many girls do not. For them, a good PE program is critical, says Mary Anne Stanton, executive director of the Center City Consortium, a program that supports at-risk, inner city Catholic elementary schools. Started in 1997, the program is a model of administration for 11 schools that are located in Washington D.C.'s poorer neighborhoods. According to Stanton, 99 percent of the schools' students are minority and 60 percent come from single parent families. "PE, art and music are the three areas which are cut when poverty is an issue," she said.

Sports are important to their whole well-being.

"For children who live at or below the poverty level, PE is a critical part of their education because they do not play after school," she continued. "They do not have the organized sports, but they can gain the exposure to sports in school."

One important part of Stanton's work is to insure that every school in the consortium has a physical education program. While it is important for both boys and girls, Stanton noted that, "For girls, if they don't have PE or engage in sports in elementary school, they are not likely to get involved in sports in high school."

Stanton herself benefited from sports when she attended the now-closed Immaculata Preparatory School on Tenley Circle in northwest D.C.

"PE brings forth a sense of pride," she said. "Sports are important to girls' basic formation. They are physical, mental and soulful beings; sports are important to their whole well-being." In addition, Stanton said, "Girls health issues are very important and are addressed through PE."

From a health standpoint, the risk of obesity and reproductive issues have been found to have a positive outcome due to sports. Regular physical activity can reduce the chances of obesity, according to the Women's Sports Foundation, while healthy lifestyles and choices also correlate with athletic endeavors.

According to a 1997 study by the National Campaign to Prevent Teen Pregnancy, teenage female athletes are less than half as likely to get pregnant as female non-athletes (5 percent and 11 percent respectively) and are more likely to report that they had never had sexual intercourse than non-athletes (54 percent and 41 percent). Teenage female athletes are also more likely to experience their first sexual intercourse later in adolescence than female non-athletes.

Moreover, sports also help girls develop a positive body image. Athletic participation allows girls to experience what their bodies can do, in contrast to the social emphasis on how girls' bodies look.

Sports and Leadership

For Mary C. Aranha, director of character education for the State of Maryland, and author of the book, *A Good Place To Be—The Guide for Leaders Who Want Their Vision to Become a Reality*, competitive sports can develop leadership skills and help children set goals.

"To be successful, you need individual and team goals. Sports prepare children for getting out into society," she said.

Aranha emphasizes the importance of sports throughout girls' lives. "Emotionally, mentally and physically, sports help girls," she said.

"Young girls can learn to be leaders through sports. Sports teach integrity and self-management by setting objective standards that girls can work to achieve.

"We all have leadership in us, and to develop that, we need to take turns being the leader and the learner," she added. This is especially important for girls, she says, since sports can give them a sense of who they are.

Blakeslee concurs. Sports, she contends, are instrumental in helping girls discover who they are and what they like. By providing an outside measure for achievement, it gives them objective standards to judge themselves and others by, she said. Leadership roles, such as being on the student council, can also help girls find a voice. "When girls put forth a proposal to do something, we do it. We let them be heard and take them seriously."

Aranha believes everyone needs "to have a part." It is what she calls inclusion, being a part of a caring community at home or school that helps to develop leadership in children.

Mary Ellen White is a part of such a community. She helps run a girls softball program in Westport, Conn. and got involved in the league in 1992, when her nephew, Jeffrey White, former chief financial officer of Major League Baseball, realized she was retired and didn't have much to do. Now, almost everything she does is softball related.

In a city like Westport, White said, "There are no neighborhoods anymore. Softball gives the girls a chance to get together and meet other people." Her two grandnieces, Erin and Colleen, both played in the league, and White has seen first hand how softball can enhance a child's self esteem. Girls, who were timid and afraid when they first start playing, begin to step forward on their own as a season develops, she reports. "For overweight girls who may be ashamed of their appearance, they learn their weight doesn't particularly matter," she said. "There is tremendous self-improvement."

Currently her grandniece, Colleen, is a top player at Staples High School in Westport and is being recruited by several colleges. In addition to softball, she is co-captain of her high school volleyball team.

Keeping Girls in Sports

As much as Title IX increased athletic opportunities for women and girls, when girls get to high school, participation in sports changes. Some girls drop sports in high school, either because of a lack of proficiency or because of the intensity of competition.

"They drop math, computer, and lots of things, not just sports," Blakeslee said. "At puberty girls get mixed messages about what is important. For boys, their bodies are a part of who they are and how they are perceived. For girls, when their bodies develop, it changes how people respond to them."

Aranha also notes that some girls are looked down upon because they are not superstars and because sports are too competitive in high school. This, she says, can affect girls' self-esteem. "Everyone is not born with the skills, but they can become skillful."

If we can keep girls in sports, Blakeslee believes it will give them confidence and strength that they can rely on throughout their lives. One way to do that, suggest Gil Reavill and Jean Zimmerman, authors of *Raising Our Athletic Daughters: How Sports Can Build Self-Esteem and Save Girls' Lives*, is to create more opportunities for girls who want to play just for the fun of it—club sports, intramural sports and junior varsity level sports.

Whether sports are played on the elite, demanding level of NCAA [National Collegiate Athletic Association] Division I programs, in elementary school or for a local sports league, girls and young women are learning goal-setting, strategic thinking and the pursuit of excellence in performance and other achievement-oriented behaviors. Gaining these skills gives the strength and confidence to pursue whatever careers they choose, says Blakeslee.

"You need to have the structures behind you, like rules of the game," she said.

"You need to practice within the rules of the game. That's one of the things sports can do."

4

Girl Athletes May Be Risking Their Health

Kristin Cobb interviewed by Mick Grant

Kristin Cobb, Ph.D, a former competitive runner, does research on the female athlete triad at Stanford University. Mick Grant is an athletic coach and respected expert in the study of child athletics.

While running can be beneficial for the health and well-being of girls, it also puts them at risk for developing the female athlete triad, a syndrome consisting of disordered eating, lack of menstrual periods, and fragile bones. Girls who run want to be thin for their sport and often restrict their calorie intake in order to obtain a lean body. However, such restriction of nutrition combined with intense burning of calories through exercise leads to insufficient production of estrogen, which results in menstrual disturbances and slow bone development—even bone loss. The longer eating disorders persist, the greater the detriment to the bones, and bone damage can never be completely reversed. Parents, coaches, and young female athletes need to be aware of the long-term consequences of combining athletics with restricted eating.

Coach Mick Grant: Dr. Cobb, We have heard more and more reports recently about the importance of female runners keeping a healthy lifestyle.

Dr. Kristin Cobb: Running can be the cornerstone of a healthy lifestyle for your child, as it prevents depression, pro-

Kristin Cobb interviewed by Mick Grant, "The Thin Line Between Healthy and At-Risk Young Runners: Advice for Preventing the 'Female Triad,' Interview with Kristin Cobb," KidsRunning.com, September 2003. Reproduced by permission of the author.

motes confidence and self-esteem, and wards off many chronic diseases. However, girls who run are at risk for a serious disorder known as the "female athlete triad," which is a combination of disordered eating, lack of menstrual periods, and fragile bones. This syndrome may lead to early osteoporosis and spontaneous fractures, prolonged psychological difficulties with weight and food, and anorexia nervosa and bulimia nervosa. The good news is that eating disorders and associated problems can be prevented, if young girls are educated about proper nutrition and encouraged to run in moderation.

The Danger of Osteoporosis

What is osteoporosis and what causes it?

Though we think of osteoporosis as an old person's disease, it is a disease that takes root in the young. Estrogen and nutrition are critical factors in a girl's bone development, and if they are not sufficient when a child is young, her bones will suffer in later life. The critical time for building the skeleton is in the early teenage years, just before and after puberty. Peak bone mass is achieved by a woman's late twenties. After this, she loses a little bone each year. Therefore, if a young girl fails to build sufficient bone in youth, she will develop thin bones (osteoporosis) much earlier in life than a woman with a healthy bone reserve.

Young women runners, who want to be lean for their sport, often restrict the amount or types of food that they eat. Meanwhile, they are burning hundreds of calories through exercise. The resulting energy drain may lead to menstrual disturbances—in trying to conserve energy, the body decreases its production of estrogen and prevents menstruation. Without sufficient estrogen and nutrition, bone development slows and bone loss may even occur.

If a girl is undernourished during the critical time when she's supposed to be building bone, these years of deprivation will be written into her skeleton, much like narrow tree rings reveal a history of drought. Though some recovery is possible, the damage can never be completely erased.

The longer disordered eating behaviors and menstrual irregularities persist, the greater the detriment to the skeleton. Some women runners in their twenties and thirties have bone strengths that would be normal for a 70- or 80-year old woman. They may spontaneously break an arm, rib, leg, hip, or vertebra. Additionally, their chance for developing a stress fracture is high.

The Importance of Good Nutrition

What are the most important components of a high performance diet? What MUST a female athlete be sure to eat and drink every day?

There is no one "magic" food that will guarantee high performance. Most importantly, young female athletes should be discouraged from restricting their diets or becoming too rigid in their food choices. Female athletes must eat enough calories every day to sustain their energy output; the calories should come from a well-balanced, varied diet that includes not only fruits and vegetables (the foods we typically think of as "healthy"), but also sufficient fat and protein. Growing girls also need to get at least 1200-1500 mg. of calcium every day. This is most easily obtained from eating 3-5 servings of dairy products, such as yogurt, milk, and cheese. Other calcium-rich foods include leafy green vegetables, such as kale, calcium-enriched juices and cereals, and tofu. A calcium supplement may be warranted if a girl gets insufficient calcium in her diet.

Bone loss can never be completely reversed, so early diagnosis and intervention is critical.

Are there negative psychological aspects of these disorders?

Beyond the physical problems, disordered eating also has adverse psychological consequences. Even after resuming menses, women recovering from the female athlete triad may still struggle with issues of food and weight. If untreated, women with the female athlete triad may also go on to develop full blown eating disorders, which have a high mortality rate. Therefore, preventing disordered eating altogether is greatly preferable to treatment after the fact.

OK, Let's talk about PREVENTING the Female Athlete Triad. How early do prevention efforts need to occur?

Girls can be at risk for developing the female athlete triad at a young age, and prevention efforts should focus on early adolescence. The majority of bone accrual occurs between the ages of 9 and 14 years. This coincides exactly with the time when girls are most at risk for developing disordered eating patterns and eating disorders. Because caloric requirements are highest when children are between 11-14 years old, restricted food intake during this period is more likely to cause energy deficiency.

Bone loss can never be completely reversed, so early diagnosis and intervention is critical. Also, it should be noted, that an analog to the female athlete triad (disordered eating, low sex steroids, and low bone strength) may exist in males, but this has not yet been established.

Prevention Through Education and Awareness

Education should aim to increase awareness of the female athlete triad and its consequences among coaches, athletes, parents, teachers, and sports physicians.

Many young women are unaware of the potential harm of restrictive eating and menstrual irregularities. In one survey of college athletes, seventy percent of the women who were engaging in pathologic weight control behaviors thought this behavior was harmless. Awareness of long-term consequences might prevent girls and women from initiating these behaviors. Young runners may be more motivated by the immediate desire to prevent stress fractures and loss of training time than by the threat of early osteoporosis (which may seem very distant to a young woman).

Pre-pubertal girls should be prepared for the fact that they are going to gain weight and body fat during puberty and that this may initially affect their performance. Education efforts should attempt to dispel the myth that thinner is always better for performance. The optimal weight, for high performance, lies somewhere in between too heavy and too thin.

Many of the nutritional messages that flood our society are geared toward the sedentary, overweight adult and promote restriction of calories and fat. These messages promote restriction of calories and fat. These messages are not appropriate for kids who are running—especially girls who should be encouraged to eat nutrient-dense foods.

I agree that an athlete doesn't want to restrict her intake of calories. What are nutrient-dense foods?

Nutrient-dense foods usually refer to foods that have a high amount of nutrients per calorie, as opposed to a food that is all sugar, for example.

The Benefits of Fat and Calories

Girls should take in adequate calories for their energy output. Eating a higher percentage of calories from fat (more fat for the same number of calories) may also help women to maintain regular menstrual periods. Adequate amounts of vitamins C, D, and K, as well as zinc and protein are also important for bone growth.

Could you more clearly describe the types of fats you recommend?

Our study did not evaluate different types of fats in terms of their efficacy in maintaining menstruation, so, in terms of promoting menstrual regularity, all fats are probably equally effective (a donut will do!). Of course, from a cardiovascular perspective, vegetable oils, nuts, avocados, and other sources of unsaturated fats are preferable to saturated fats.

Is there a formula for calculating adequate calorie intake?

There are calculators that can be used to estimate basal metabolic rate (based on weight, body frame size and age, plus energy expended from activity (based on the type and intensity of activity). You may be able to find one of these formulas on various on-line diet sites, but a single formula may not work well for children and teens because it depends so much on their stage of growth. The US RDA [recommended daily allowance] recommends about 2200 kcal per day for normal 11–18 year old girls, but this does not factor in added activity such as running. A rough guideline is to add 100 kcal per mile run per day.

While eating enough calcium (1500 mg/day) is important for bone development, eating calcium-rich foods is not sufficient to ensure bone health. Estrogen is also a key factor in building strong bones, and excess calcium will not prevent bone loss in a woman who is not menstruating or is undernourished.

How could we educate parents and athletes to ensure the proper balance of estrogen? Could you explain how to manage this?

Estrogen balance is hard to monitor other than making sure that a woman is menstruating regularly (or gets her first period on time). Estrogen should be normal if a woman is eating right, but it's hard to give advice beyond this.

High-impact exercise stimulates bone growth in children, particularly if it occurs before puberty. Therefore, exercise in childhood can help maximize peak bone density. Jumping puts higher forces on bone and stimulates more bone growth than running. Young runners should be encouraged to add jumping exercises and sports that involve jumping, such as basketball, soccer, and gymnastics, to their fitness routine.

Warning Signs for the Female Athlete Triad

Some signs of disordered eating are:

- In older girls, delayed menarche (first period) and missed menstrual periods

- Restrictive eating behaviors; avoidance of certain foods

- Secretive eating

- Sudden weight loss or failure to make normal weight goals for age

- Obsession with food and/or weight

- Excessive exercise

- Signs of purging

Signs of low bone strength:

- In older girls, delayed menarche (first period) and missed menstrual periods

- Stress fractures can be a sign of low bone strength.

- A bone density test is the best way to determine bone strength.

As a parent or coach, what types of annual testing would you recommend? Is there a link between low iron and these problems?

A yearly bone density test is not necessary for most young women. A bone density test would only be recommended for women who have amenorrhea, fractures, or an overt eating disorder.

Low iron may reflect nutritional deficiencies, but low iron per se does not have a large effect on bone health.

5

Athletics in Schools Helps Prevent Childhood Obesity

The Center for Health and Health Care in Schools

The staff and consultants at the Center for Health and Health Care in Schools explore ways to strengthen the well-being of children through health programs and health care services in schools. The Center is part of the School for Public Health and Health Services at George Washington University Medical Center.

Studies have shown that, since 1996, childhood obesity has increased to such a dangerous level that more than 9 million youngsters are now overweight. One of the leading causes of this epidemic is a marked decline in physical activity and athletic participation. Because many children are not involved in after-school sports, schools should make it a priority that their students receive adequate physical education classes that promote lifelong habits of physical activity.

The "calories in" part of the "calories in-calories out" formula for managing overweight in children got special attention last month [May 2006], in the form of a policy statement on active healthy living for children from the American Academy of Pediatrics (AAP) and a once-in-five-years report from the National Association of Sport and Physical Education on what states do and do not mandate for school physical education.

The Center for Health and Health Care in Schools, "The Shape of the Nation's Children," *Center E-journal: Health and Health Care in Schools*, vol. 7, June–July 2006. www.healthinschools.org/ejournal/2006/june3.htm. Reproduced by permission.

Both reports pointed out that it is hard to ignore childhood overweight, which has increased exponentially in the past decade, to the point that 16 percent of children between the ages of 6 and 19 years are now overweight. That is more than 9 million young people, the National Association noted; and the AAP called the situation "an epidemic driven by multiple factors," among them marked declines in the amount of physical activity children engage in, both in school and out of school.

Schools Need to Improve Physical Education Classes

In its policy statement, "Active Healthy Living: Prevention of Childhood Obesity Through Increased Physical Activity," the American Academy of Pediatrics [AAP] urged pediatric health care providers and public health officials to advocate for increased physical activity for children and teenagers in a number of ways, including improving access to physical education at school on a daily basis. The Academy notes that schools alone cannot solve the overweight and obesity crisis, but since children spend most of their waking hours at school, "the availability of regular physical activity in that setting is critical."

A study in 2000 found that only 8 percent of American elementary schools, 6.4 percent of middle schools, and 5.8 percent of high schools with existing physical education requirements actually provided daily PE classes for all grades for the entire year. Add to that the fact that a poll of parents of children 9 to 13 years old found that 61.5 percent of the youngsters did not participate in any organized physical activities after school and 22.6 percent didn't engage in non-organized physical activity after school hours, and you have a picture of across-the-board inactivity, both in school and out, the AAP pointed out.

And while physical activity needs to be promoted at home and in the community, "school is perhaps the most encompassing way for all children to benefit," the AAP said. The policy statement noted that there is an opportunity for pediatricians to get involved with school districts on this issue, under a federal revision of child nutrition programs that calls for every school receiving funding from the National School Lunch and Breakfast Programs to develop a local wellness policy by the beginning of the 2006–2007 school year, with goals for physical activity as well as nutrition. "In light of the school wellness policy, many schools are looking to modify their present PE programs to improve physical activity standards," the policy statement said.

The AAP policy statement is critical of past physical education programs that used calisthenics and acquisition of sports-specific skills to promote fitness. Instead, the statement calls for curricula and instruction that emphasize knowledge, attitudes, and motor and behavioral skills required to adopt and maintain lifelong habits of physical activity. That could include aerobics and strength training, the report suggests, and walking and dancing.

Among the most difficult but most important challenges in an effort to increase childhood physical activity are making exercise alternatives as attractive, exciting, and enjoyable as video games; convincing school boards that PE and other school-based physical activities are as important to long-term productivity as are academics; and engineering physical environments to promote physical activity, the AAP concluded.

In its first report since 2000, the National Association for Sport and Physical Education gave states and the federal government a failing grade on physical education in the American school system. Noting that no federal law requires that physical education be offered in schools or provides any incentive for physical education programs, the report says states too are dodging the issue, with many setting some general or minimum requirements but delegating responsibility for meeting those standards to individual school districts.

[P]hysical education . . . has become a lower priority.

In detailed tables put together during the winter of 2006, the Association in cooperation with the American Heart Association reported on the status of physical education in each state and the District of Columbia in the areas of:

- time requirements;

- exemptions, waivers, and substitutions;

- class size;

- standards, curriculum, and instruction for physical education;

- student assessment and program accountability;

- physical education teacher certification and licensure;

- national board certification in physical education;

- whether there is a state physical education coordinator; and

- whether the state requires collection of body mass index (BMI) data.

State profiles of what is currently required in each of those areas show that while most states mandate physical education, most do not require a specific amount of instructional time, and about half allow exemptions, waivers, and/or substitutions, loopholes that the report notes "significantly reduce the effectiveness of the mandate." And even within states there are "very diverse patterns of delivery" of physical education, as the result of commitment to local control of education, which leaves specific decisions regarding time, class size, and student assessment to local school districts or even schools.

Physical Activity Is Losing Out

At the federal level, the report notes that five years after a U.S. Surgeon General's Call to Action to Prevent and Decrease Overweight and Obesity put forth quality daily K–12 physical education as key action, a federal law, the No Child Left Behind Act, is actually threatening the amount of time available for physical education, with schools concentrating on assessing student achievement in defined core academic subjects. "As states conduct standardized tests to hold schools and students accountable, content that is not tested, such as physical education, has become a lower priority."

In one surprising development, the survey found that almost one-fourth of states now allow required physical education credits to be earned through what the report calls "online physical education courses." Of the 12 states (Alaska, Connecticut, Florida, Indiana, Kentucky, Minnesota, New Hampshire, North Dakota, Oregon, South Carolina, Utah, and Virginia) with online options, six offer comprehensive physical education (defined as addressing all state and national standards), five offer online personal fitness/wellness courses, and two offer online sports and weight training courses. In six of the states, all students are allowed to take the courses; in others, students must request permission and be approved.

6

Playing Football Can Encourage Obesity

Todd Dvorak

Todd Dvorak is a writer for the Associated Press.

College and professional football players are known for their huge size and muscle mass, often weighing as much as 300 pounds. Now, according to a January 2007 study, the trend toward bigger and beefier has filtered down to football players at the high school level. Researchers at Iowa State University found that of the high school players analyzed, 45 percent were overweight and 9 percent were considered severely obese. Because overweight children and teens face higher risks for heart disease, high blood pressure, and diabetes, health experts are concerned about this trend toward obesity in young football players.

IOWA CITY, Iowa - Heavy tackles and 300-pound nose guards are common in pro and college football. Now a study shows the trend toward beefier, overweight linemen is emerging at the high school level.

Researchers at Iowa State University found nearly half of the offensive and defensive linemen playing on Iowa high school teams qualify as overweight, and one in 10 meet medical standards for severe obesity.

"These are 15- and 16-year-old boys that have a weight and body-mass ... that as they enter adulthood puts many at a very adverse health condition," said Dr. Joe Eisenmann, co-author of the study and a professor in pediatric exercise physiology at Iowa State.

The study appears in Wednesday's [January 24, 2007] *Journal of the American Medical Association.*

For years at the pro and college level, teams have sought bigger, stronger linemen who are harder to budge. Players have responded by adding weight and muscle mass, making the 300-pound lineman fairly common, sports medical experts said.

Recently, however, the National Football League [NFL] and players have taken greater note of health risks for heavy athletes because of two high-profile NFL player deaths and a 2005 study, which concluded that 56 percent of NFL players fit medical standards for obesity.

The size, bulk and ever-widening girth of the pros apparently has not gone unnoticed by those dreaming of one day playing at the next level.

"Sure I look at college players and pro players a lot and size them up," said Chad Wilson, a junior who started at center last season for Iowa City West High School. He wants to add at least another 20 pounds before next season.

Pressure to get bigger, stronger, heavier may come from parents and coaches, but there is also a desire from within, players said.

"You want to have the weight to be able to compete in the conference we're in," said Thomas Reynolds, a junior linebacker hoping to switch to the defensive line next season.

The study's researchers began by gathering height and weight data of 3,686 varsity linemen available from rosters from all classes of Iowa high school football teams. They used that data to calculate a body-mass index, the same tool used for the NFL study.

Of the players analyzed, 28 percent were deemed at risk of being overweight and 45 percent fit the standards for being overweight, including 9 percent who met adult severe obesity standards.

Researchers believe the study is one of the first—and most comprehensive—appraisals of obesity in high school football.

"We don't suspect, though, that Iowa is unique in any way," said Kelly Laurson, a graduate assistant and co-author of the study. "I suspect that states with an even richer high school football tradition, like Florida and Texas, may have an even bigger problem."

But the researchers and sports medicine experts acknowledge the study is not perfect.

The roster data was obtained in the preseason before athletes had a chance to get in shape, and the BMI formula can, in some cases, be deceptive, they said.

Dr. Edward Wojtys, an orthopedic surgeon and chief at the University of Michigan Sports Medicine Service, said the BMI fails to account for muscle mass and lean tissue and is less accurate than more sophisticated measuring techniques.

"On the other hand, there is still an obvious and growing problem of obesity among football linemen," Wojtys said.

"The rules have changed in ways that favor larger and larger-sized bodies rather than smaller, athletic ones. It's not a good trend and one we should be concerned about."

Health experts also said the results are no surprise in a society dealing with high rates of child and adolescent obesity. Overweight children and teens face higher risks for heart disease, high blood pressure, diabetes and weight problems through adulthood.

They said it's impossible to lay blame on any single source or factor.

"But I think if we're honest about it, at least in this case, we'd have to look at the role models for these young athletes," said Dr. George Phillips, a pediatrician at the University of Iowa's Sports Medicine Center.

"Most of these kids aren't going to play professionally or even at the college level. So what we need to do is to make sure if they're going to add weight, muscle mass, that they do it in a healthy way."

7

Child Athletes Need a Healthy Diet

TeensHealth

TeensHealth is part of the award-winning KidsHealth Web resource, providing doctor-approved information about children's health through adolescence. KidsHealth was created and is supported by the Nemours Foundation's Center for Children's Health Media.

Young athletes expend a tremendous amount of energy in their sports; without plenty of fuel—derived from calories and good nutrition—to provide that energy, their performance and growth will suffer. In order to get all the nutrients they need, athletes should eat a variety of foods, including lean meats, dairy products, whole grains, fruits and vegetables, and unsaturated fats. Also, athletes should be wary of supplements. Instead of helping the body, salt tablets, hormonal supplements like creatine, and anabolic steroids can cause serious physical and mental damage. Furthermore, athletes must remember that drinking water is just as important as food to maintain a healthy body and reach maximum performance.

A Guide to Eating for Sports

There's a lot more to eating for sports than chowing down on carbs or chugging sports drinks. The good news is that eating to reach your peak performance level likely doesn't require a special diet or supplements. It's all about working the right foods into your fitness plan in the right amounts. Here are some basics.

Eat Extra for Excellence

Teen athletes have unique nutrition needs. Because athletes work out more than their less-active peers, they generally need extra calories to fuel both their sports performance *and* their growth. Depending on how active they are, teen athletes may need anywhere from 2,000 to 5,000 total calories per day to meet their energy needs.

So what happens if teen athletes don't eat enough? Their bodies are less likely to achieve peak performance and may even break down rather than build up muscles. Athletes who don't take in enough calories every day won't be as fast and as strong as they could be. And extreme calorie restriction could lead to growth problems and other serious health risks for both girls and guys.

Since teen athletes need extra fuel, it's usually a bad idea for them to diet. Athletes in sports where weight is emphasized—such as wrestling, swimming, dance, or gymnastics—may feel pressure to lose weight, but they need to weigh that choice with the possible negative side effects mentioned above. If a coach, gym teacher, or teammate says that you need to go on a diet, talk to your doctor first or visit a dietitian who specializes in teen athletes. If a health professional you trust agrees that it's safe to diet, he or she can work with you to develop a plan that allows you to perform your best and lose weight.

Eat a Variety of Foods

You may have heard about "carb loading" before a game. But when it comes to powering your game for the long haul, it's a bad idea to focus on only one type of food. Carbohydrates are an important source of fuel, but they're only one of many foods an athlete needs. It also takes vitamins, minerals, protein, and fats to stay in peak playing shape.

Muscular Minerals and Vital Vitamins

Calcium helps build the strong bones that athletes depend on, and iron carries oxygen to muscles. Most teens don't get enough of these minerals, and that's especially true of teen athletes because their needs may be even higher than those of other teens.

Anabolic steroids can seriously mess with a person's hormones. . . .

To get the iron you need, eat lean red meats (meats with not much fat on them); grains that are fortified with iron; and green, leafy vegetables. Calcium—a must for protecting against stress fractures—is found in dairy foods, such as low-fat milk, yogurt, and cheese.

In addition to calcium and iron, you need a whole bunch of other vitamins and minerals that do everything from help you access energy to keep you from getting sick. Eating a balanced diet, including lots of different fruits and veggies, should provide the vitamins and minerals needed for good health and sports performance.

Protein Power

Athletes need slightly more protein than less-active teens, but most teen athletes get plenty of protein through regular eating. It's a myth that athletes need a huge daily intake of protein to build large, strong muscles. Muscle growth comes from regular training and hard work—not popping a pill. And taking in too much protein can actually harm the body, causing dehydration, calcium loss, and even kidney problems.

Good sources of protein are fish, lean meats and poultry, eggs, dairy, nuts, soy, and peanut butter.

Carb Charger

Carbohydrates provide athletes with an excellent source of fuel. Cutting back on carbs or following low-carb diets isn't a good idea for athletes because restricting carbohydrates can cause a person to feel tired and worn out, which ultimately affects performance.

Nutrition experts advise people to choose whole grains (such as brown rice, oatmeal, sweet potatoes, whole wheat bread, and starchy vegetables like corn and peas) more often than their more processed counterparts like white rice and white bread. That's because whole grains provide both the energy athletes need to perform and the fiber and other nutrients they need to be healthy. Sugary carbs such as candy bars or sodas are less healthy for athletes because they don't contain any of the other nutrients you need. In addition, eating candy bars or other sugary snacks just before practice or competition can give athletes a quick burst of energy and then leave them to "crash" or run out of energy before they've finished working out.

Fat Fuel

Everyone needs a certain amount of fat each day, and this is particularly true for athletes. That's because active muscles quickly burn through carbs and need fats for long-lasting energy. Like carbs, not all fats are created equal. Experts advise athletes to concentrate on healthier fats, such as the unsaturated fat found in most vegetable oils. Choosing when to eat fats is also important for athletes. Fatty foods can slow digestion, so it's a good idea to avoid eating these foods for a few hours before and after exercising.

Shun Supplements

Protein supplements and energy bars don't do a whole lot of good, but they won't really do you much harm either. But other types of supplements can really do some damage.

Anabolic steroids can seriously mess with a person's hormones, causing side effects like testicular shrinkage and baldness in guys and facial hair growth in girls. Steroids can cause mental health problems, including depression and serious mood swings. Some over-the-counter supplements contain hormones that are related to testosterone (such as dehydroepiandrosterone, or DHEA for short). These supplements have similar side effects to anabolic steroids. These and other sports supplements (like creatine, for example) have not been tested in people younger than 18. So the risks of taking them are not yet known.

Salt tablets are another supplement to watch out for. People take them to avoid dehydration, but salt tablets can actually lead a person to become dehydrated. In large amounts, salt can cause nausea, vomiting, cramps, and diarrhea and may damage the lining of the stomach. In general, you are better off drinking fluids in order to maintain hydration. Any salt you lose in sweat can usually be made up in one normal meal after exercise.

Ditch Dehydration

Speaking of dehydration, water is just as important to unlocking your game power as food. When you sweat during exercise, it's easy to become overheated, headachy, and worn out—especially in hot or humid weather. Even mild dehydration can affect an athlete's physical and mental performance.

There's no one-size-fits-all formula for how much water to drink. How much fluid each person needs depends on the individual's age, size, level of physical activity, and environmental temperature.

Experts recommend that athletes drink before and after exercise as well as every 15 to 20 minutes during exercise. In general, most athletes need 1-2 cups prior to exercise and 1/2 to 1 cup every 15 to 20 minutes throughout exercise. Don't wait until you feel thirsty, because thirst is a sign that your body has needed liquids for a while. But don't force yourself to drink more fluids than you may need either. It's hard to run when there's a lot of water sloshing around in your stomach!

If you like the taste of sports drinks better than regular water, then it's OK to drink them. But it's important to know that a sports drink is really no better for you than water unless you are exercising for more than 90 minutes or in really hot weather. The additional carbohydrates and electrolytes may improve performance in these conditions, but otherwise your body will do just as well with water.

Avoid drinking carbonated drinks or juice because they could give you a stomachache while you're competing.

Caffeine

Drinks that contain caffeine, including some soft drinks, tea, and coffee, may contribute to dehydration. Although some studies have found that caffeine may help with endurance sports performance, it's good to weigh any benefits against potential problems. Too much caffeine can leave an athlete feeling anxious or jittery. It can also cause trouble sleeping. All of these can drag down a person's sports performance. Plus, taking certain medications—including supplements—can make caffeine's side effects seem even worse.

Game Dat Eats

Most of your body's energy on game day will come from the foods you've eaten over the past several days. But you can boost your performance even more by paying attention to the food you eat on game day. Strive for a game-day diet rich in carbohydrates, moderate in protein, and low in fat. Here are some guidelines on what to eat and when:

- **Eat a meal 2 to 4 hours before the game or event**: Combine a serving of low-fiber fruit or vegetable (such as juice, plums, melons, cherries, or peaches) with a protein and carbohydrate meal (like a turkey or chicken sandwich, cereal and milk, or chicken noodle soup and yogurt).

- **Eat a snack less than 2 hours before the game**: If you haven't had time to have a pre-game meal, be sure to have a light snack such as crackers, a bagel, or low-fat yogurt.

It's a good idea to avoid eating anything for the hour before you compete or have practice because digestion requires energy—energy that you want to use to win. Also, eating too soon before any kind of activity can leave food in the stomach, making you feel full, bloated, crampy, and sick. Everyone is different, so get to know what works best for you. You may want to experiment with meal timing and how much to eat on practice days so that you are better prepared for game day.

Want to get an eating plan personalized for you? The U.S. government has developed a website, MyPyramid, that tells a person how much to eat from different food groups based on age, gender, and activity level.

8

Working Out Builds Self-Esteem in Children

Jake Steinfeld

Chairman of Body by Jake Enterprises, Jake Steinfeld is a leader in fitness products and provides information about living a healthy lifestyle.

The secret to success begins with believing in one's own potential; however, many young people do not feel very self-confident. One great way to develop self-confidence is to work out and train with weights. The physical and emotional benefits of working out—such as a muscular, healthy body and a feeling of achievement and control—will be obvious in a very short time, which will in turn lead to other people's respect and admiration. Working out can set into motion the cycle of attaining self-assurance, maximizing potential, reaching goals, and ultimately finding fulfillment and success.

Ask the Tough Questions . . . of Yourself!

Take a good long look in a mirror. If that makes you uneasy, I'm thrilled! You're looking at yourself honestly. If you truly want to improve yourself, it's crucial that you examine what it is about you that needs work. The physical shortcomings will probably leap out at you first—maybe a flabby mid-section, stick-thin legs, or no-show biceps. However, I'm more interested in how you feel and think right now. Change the inside before the outside, and success will come much more quickly—in both camps!

Are you happy with your life right now? Do you think you're headed in a positive direction? What challenges are you meeting well? Are there any that are getting the better of you? How do you view yourself? Do others look at you the same way? If there's a difference, why? Of the character traits that you don't like, why do you think they exist? Has each trait improved or gotten worse over time?

If you feel as if you are perpetually having to prove yourself, maybe it's because you doubt your own abilities. If you are easily annoyed by people or things, perhaps you are always irritable. If you sense that you can never satisfy other people, the truth might be that you rarely satisfy yourself!

Few guys are brave enough—and patient enough—to answer these questions or face their conclusions. Just like a good medical checkup, only if you know what ails you can you get better. You must reckon with exactly who you are right now, for better or worse. Then you will know exactly what you need to work on. If you're struggling with seeing exactly who you are or think there are some problematic elements in you that you may not be consciously aware of, ask a good friend who is willing to answer questions about you in a frank way. Just don't get angry at him or her afterward if the answers are more brutal than you'd like—they're supposed to help!

Most people want to be told only how great they are— how funny, smart, and good-looking. That, however, prevents growth. If you want to reach your full potential, you need to listen to criticism and perhaps even seek it out. You have to be able to like that person you see in the mirror. No matter how many flaws you (or your pal) detect or how low you've sunk, only if you are kind to yourself will life do you any favors!

So please don't beat yourself up anymore. The game has not even begun for you. You're still in the on-deck circle. By the time you get to the plate, armed with my workout training and helpful thoughts, you will be able to hit one out of the park almost every time! To do that, you must feel good about yourself, because when you do, others will feel good about you as well. All the successful people I have trained in Hollywood are comfortable with themselves, and this is one of their many secrets of their success. After all, how can you expect other people to appreciate you unless you do?

There's a tremendous satisfaction that comes from knowing that you do everything you can to maximize your potential.

Before I looked in the mirror, I wasn't exactly on a hot streak. My fortunes with sports, girls, and schoolwork were all heading south. Starting to train, however, reversed these fortunes by 180 degrees. I didn't strike gold in all these things instantly, but success was ensured because I had begun to tackle each problem area of my life. Behind my stuttering self was a smooth, powerful talker; inside my round, underachieving body was a muscular athlete. I was just waiting to emerge! I had serious potential, and weight training brought it out. . . .

The person who knows best what you are capable of, however, is you—no matter what anybody else says about you. Even if you are written off by someone who thinks you'll never fulfill your promise, it's up to you to prove that person wrong.

A lot of people who knew me when I was growing up didn't think I'd amount to much. They certainly didn't predict that I would become a successful entrepreneur, "trainer to the stars," founder of a professional sports league, and so on. Heck, they didn't even see me as team captain on the basketball team. But if I'd listened to them, I wouldn't be able to list any of those accomplishments.

Your potential is in your hands. No matter how great a father and mother you have, how smart a teacher, how skilled a coach, nobody can tap your potential the way you can. Soaking up all of their wisdom and encouragement will help, but ultimately you are the master of your own potential. When I picked up that very first weight, it was a moment that I'll never forget. I suddenly felt the surge of potential from within. I saw muscles, a beautiful woman (who turned out to be my wife, Tracey!), financial success, happiness—all within range.

Once I got on top of the training, everything else began to improve.

The same can happen to you. You too will notice that your potential is truly unlimited if you let your imagination roam and put plenty of work and know-how behind it. There's a tremendous satisfaction that comes from knowing that you do everything you can to maximize your potential in everything you try. What's more, you'll have no regrets! . . .

One Thing Leads to Many Others

It's well known that a good education opens worlds for you, but did you know that training does the same? Training put into motion everything in my life that wouldn't budge—my weight problem, stuttering, bad grades, and failure with girls. I quickly knew that great things were around the corner. First I felt and saw my muscles grow as my fat disappeared; then people began to treat me differently. The self-confidence that had eluded me for so long was now a part of me.

Amazingly, once I got on top of the training, everything else began to improve, while all the hard work I put into workouts made everything else easier to deal with. Getting up in the morning, walking down the school hallway holding my head up, outdueling my competitors in my chosen sport—in all these areas, I experienced tremendous progress. The fact that eventually I could switch from the baggy shirts that used to camouflage my round body to form-fitting ones illustrates perfectly just how far I had come.

In very little time, people started to notice that I was no longer that chubby Jake who couldn't be taken seriously. I'll never forget the first comment I got about my new physique, when one of the guys told me, "Yo, Jake, what's with the biceps, man? You been workin' out or whaat?" Topping that was a girl who touched my arm and said, "Ohhh, Jake, you've got muscles!" I was already motivated, but these positive reinforcements fueled me even further. You, too, will receive many compliments after you begin to make some impressive changes—and if you're like I was and never had heard these sorts of compliments before, they'll make you prouder than you've been in a long time, maybe ever!

Before long, I had an image that I wanted to maintain, and even build on—and make my previous bloated image history! Every night in my basement, I chipped away at my fat and added a little more muscle. It was what I looked forward to most each day. Becoming stronger and more muscular became my passion—one that has never died! I couldn't get enough of anything in the media that had to do with it, from the Hercules movies to the body-building magazines.

I don't know how training will change *you* but there's no doubt that it will. Wait until you see what happens! You'll bring this new sense of power over your life to everything you do, and then you'll realize that you have the power to alter whatever you choose. Training will put you into the driver's seat of your life.

Get Naked!

I'm talking about getting naked in both respects—mental and physical—when you begin to train. Dig up all your weaknesses and problems while you work out and, one by one, wipe them away as you push your body with the weights. Training has a way of stripping you to the core, if it's done right. It's funny: you walk out of a workout feeling completely relaxed and refreshed—even though you're pumped and sweaty!

Once you start to feel good about yourself, everybody else will feel good about you, too: your parents, brothers and sisters, friends, teachers, coaches. You'll probably thump your forehead and ask yourself, "Why didn't I do this earlier!" Why? Because you refused to get naked!

There are so many reasons why: being glued to the tube or stuck on the Web for hours every day; family members who view exercise as an expression of mania: friends who can't be dragged to the gym, yet are game for a cigarette anytime; your own problem with drugs or alcohol; the misconception that working out is just for jocks; the idea that preparing for college and life is only about hitting the books; the belief that training requires tons of time.

I challenge you to put down the remote control, the mouse, and the phone, and start heaving some weights. You'll still have time to press and double-click, but now your time will be more focused. I challenge you to put down the French fries and soda, and instead, eat and drink what will make strong. (Don't worry, you'll see in Chapter 9 that one day a week you can eat whatever you choose!) I challenge you to drop the attitude that will keep you away from your workouts and to substitute an attitude of excitement with which to greet every training session.

9

Academics Should Not Be Neglected in Favor of Sports

Eddie Griffin

Eddie Griffin is a freelance writer who does monthly opinion columns for the Dawgs' Bite, *Mississippi State's Web site focusing on team sports.*

Excelling at sports is exciting and rewarding and should be encouraged, but not at the expense of academics. It is easy to get caught up in the idea of becoming a professional athlete with the huge income and rich lifestyle that go along with it. Realistically, however, only a small percentage of aspiring players actually succeed; what future lies ahead for those who do not? Parents, teachers, coaches, and especially student athletes themselves need to understand that "winning at all costs" diminishes lives. Receiving an education should be the top priority.

Every year, numerous talented players miss out on the chance to play top-level football because of failure to meet academic requirements. We all know that it happens, because as fans we hear and see that all-state linebacker who doesn't play a down for our team because he didn't pass his geography class.

But do we recognize it for the problem that it really is? It's no secret that football players are pretty low on the list when it comes to academic prowess. There are plenty who get the job done without skirting it too close, and plenty have their smarts, but far too many have academic issues, for one reason or another.

It's a problem that's deeply rooted and starts to manifest itself long before high school in many cases. Accountability for it doesn't fall on only one party. It has to be shared on many levels.

Parents Should Stress Education

First of all, you have to start with the parents/guardians. Credit should be given to the many parents who do their utmost to help their child get their education, but it's not the same for all. Most reasonable parents have the best of intentions for their children, but some of them get as caught up or, in some cases, even more caught up in the fact that their child is such a talent on the playing field that they forget that they need to make sure he knows his ABCs and 123s. Others are just out and out selfish and simply push him too hard to lower that 40 time another tenth or bust it in the weight room for an extra hour instead of spending that hour studying for his English test. It's all well and good to want to see your child succeed. Even the parents who only care just a little bit do, but it doesn't need to be at the expense of their future.

If you're a parent, here's a sobering (or at least it should be) possibility to ponder: After he fails to make the grade and misses out on playing at USC, simply because he has the reading skills of an elementary student, there's a good chance he may well be living at home much longer than you really want him to.

Coaches and Teachers Should Insist on Education

Second of all, you have to look at how much the coaches push their players to get it done off the field as much as they do on it. Some coaches are pretty strict and walk the straight and narrow when it comes to making sure their players get it done in the classroom. No one wants their star back to miss the big game because he's academically ineligible. But on that same token, some coaches resort to getting the teachers to give their stars a break in the classroom so they can slip by and be able to play. It brings a new meaning to the phrase "winning at all costs," because it can do a lot to cost Mr. Fivestar a shot at a realistic future outside of sports.

That being said, if a teacher goes along with that kind of behavior, that's compromising their position. Teachers are supposed to help their students learn, not let them slide because someone tells them to. Some teachers, just as they do with regular students, don't bother to give the student-athletes the classroom help they need, giving way to a mindset of "Oh, they're just dumb as rocks already. There's nothing I can do to help them." That not only defies their duties as a teacher, it also lays the path for a poor future for Mr. Fivestar and some of his teammates.

Responsibility Lies with the Student Athlete

But, however much responsibility lies with other parties, the majority of it lies with the student-athlete himself. Ultimately, despite the influences of anyone else, it's up to him to get the job done. And really, compared to 'regular' students, he has to do less work to get just as far.

The NCAA minimum eligibility requirements are not the same as the normal admissions requirements for many schools, which gives ol' Johnny Fivestar a little wiggle room. The NCAA currently uses a sliding scale, which means that a player can get into school with a lower GPA, provided he gets the right ACT score, or vice versa. The scales balance at a 2.5 GPA on the core courses (there are fourteen core credits you have to take and pass, according to the current NCAA requirements for Division I) and a 17 on the ACT (or its equivalent on the SAT). A 2.5 GPA equates to a little more than a C average, which is pretty doable if you put in the work in most of your classes, even if there are a few Ds scattered about your transcript. As far as the ACT goes, a 17 is a few points below the national average, so it's also doable. Even if you falter on one part, you can make up for it by doing well on others.

True enough, there are plenty of regular students who can't meet those requirements. Some people have problems with learning. Some people just don't care enough. But if you don't have problems with learning, and you have full mental capacity, there is little excuse for you to fall short. If you know you need to hit a target, you will do everything in your power to make sure you do.

Sometimes circumstances get in the way, but that's where willpower and motivation come in. You have to rise above it if you know you have to. Plenty of people have legitimate reasons for messing up, but after a while, even good reasons just become excuses. If you can at least show you care and that you're capable of doing well, it'll prove to the college coaches going after you that you're worth going after, even if you may have had some issues in the past. That comes from a former head coach who's had to deal with his share of recruits.

Schools Offer Resources for Learning

Most high schools do plenty to ensure that their students know what they need to do in order to not only get their high school diploma, but also what they need in case they want to go to a four-year college. I graduated high school in 2003, and I remember how from middle school onwards, we regularly did homeroom work that told us what we needed to know. We had a folder that held information like test scores, schedules, and academic requirements. That folder followed us from middle school to high school. Not only that, but before each year of high school, we had to fill out our schedules and look at what we had and hadn't taken already and what we needed to take. If we didn't know something, the guidance counselor was there to advise us.

Every school may not do those things the same way mine did, but some sort of graduation and post-graduation prep work is done, and there are guidance counselors there to help out as well.

Football does take up a lot of time, and you do take a lot of hits to the head, but there are no excuses for not knowing what you need to do to graduate or to meet the standards at the next level. Here's a simple equation for you. Players have to learn dozens of plays in a playbook. They do so by practice and repetition. Learning in the classroom takes that too. It may seem too time-consuming to have to devote time to both, but there are more than enough hours in the day.

Also, when it comes to standardized tests, schools do prep work for that, and there are practice booklets available at schools, in bookstores, and online to help; besides that, there are also plenty of tutors out there. But, a 6'4", 250 guy who can go and play on a broken hand may not have the strength to go and ask a 5'5", 120 pounds soaking wet 'nerd' for help to get that qualifying score on his ACT. And you can't use the excuse, 'but I have to practice or go lift weights' too much, because you can miss or reschedule a couple of weightlifting sessions to go make sure you get your grades.

So, the resources are out there. Once again, no excuses. Sure, a child may not always think rationally on his own, but if you have full brain capacity, and you know you need to do something, it's on you if you don't go and do all you can to accomplish it. If you need to pull your ACT score up a few points, get a tutor. And even for the student-athletes who have learning disabilities, they can get help for that too. The unfortunate thing is, they may be too ashamed to admit it, and even if everyone does know, it may be getting covered up.

Education Is Important To Be Successful in Life

That leads to one of the biggest issues. It'd be pretty naive to ignore the fact that athletes tend to get breaks and passes that many regular students don't get. These practices not only hurt the athletes who actually do put the work in to make the grades and help to further the 'dumb jock' stereotype, but it also is a slap in the face of the educational system and those regular students who actually have to fall back on their educations. It doesn't happen near as much as it did maybe two or three decades ago when someone like my mother was still in school, but I've seen firsthand that it still does.

Does it really help the athlete in the long run? Far from it. Sooner or later, their ignorance will be exposed. Maybe they'll get breaks on through college and squeak by enough to get a degree or play professionally, but when they have to go sign a contract or be out in the real world, they'll be lost. Or maybe their inability to read well or do simple math catches up to them in college, and they're much too far behind to be able to catch up.

Some will wise up and put in the work they need to so they can make their grades, but so many others are too engrained in laziness to turn things around, and they wind up on a completely different path than they'd hoped.

Yes, kids can be easily swayed by what they see on TV and by what people around them whisper in their ear. For those who do try to sway them in the wrong direction, you should be ashamed of yourselves. If you really care, you'd get through to them that they need their education more than that 4.3 40 to impress the scouts and recruiters. But, it's a two-way street. Through that immature young adult brain, the student-athlete needs to see for himself and decide on his own what he needs to do. Ultimately, it's up to him. Sure, many have legitimate reasons to suffer a lapse academically, but most of those reasons wear out after a time and become nothing more than excuses.

The fact is that most of the stories we hear of players failing to meet academic requirements involve black athletes. A good number of these guys come from less than stellar backgrounds, and that can play into their thought process. "Why do I need an education? The easiest way to get me and my family out of here is if I work as hard as I can to make it to the NFL. I don't want to be stuck working 9 to 5 on some dead-end job. I want to be making millions. I need to."

Athletes Need a Back-up Plan

It's easy for a teenager to be disillusioned by seeing the enormous contracts and lavish lifestyles the Michael Vick's and others like him lead. Michael Vick [professional football player] came from one of the rougher neighborhoods in the country, along with [professional athletes] Aaron Brooks, Allen Iverson, and Ronald Curry. But for all of those guys, there's a Marcus Vick or Maurice Clarett [football players involved with illegal activities]. You have to think realistically. The money, cars, women, and fame are all nice to daydream about, but you have to have a backup plan.

Only a small percentage of the players you see on college rosters right now will actually ever make it to the NFL. Plenty of those who don't go on to have futures elsewhere, some in a football-related capacity. But what becomes of that guy who let his education fall by the wayside? What can he or anyone else do? Just look back and see how little reason there is for Johnny Former-Fivestar to be flipping burgers or sweeping floors, forced to reminisce about that one-handed, game-winning TD [touchdown] catch in the state championship game or that time he knocked out Mr. Future All-Pro's mouthpiece, instead of being out there doing well for himself and living with no regrets.

Unfortunately, these problems have their roots long before high school. A lot of these guys have already been long left behind or given up before they get to high school or to the point where they see they have potential to play at a higher level.

It doesn't have to happen. There are far too many academic casualties, athlete-related and otherwise. For anyone who is in a position to help prevent it, do everything in your power to. Coaches, teachers, parents, it's on you. And to the students themselves, your education is important, more important than that next touchdown you score or that interception you made to save the last game. Football comes to an end sooner or later.

The future isn't a game. But to look at it in football terms, when it's all said and done, we don't want to see Johnny Five-star on the wrong end of the scoreline on the playing field of the real world.

10

Athletic Participation Builds Confidence in Disabled Children

Kyle Maynard

Athlete, inspirational speaker, and author, Kyle Maynard was born without developed arms and legs. Nonetheless, he participated in several sports, including swimming, baseball, street hockey, football, and wrestling.

Succeeding in athletics is a great way for young people to build confidence and self-esteem, a fact that also holds true for disabled children. With enough determination and commitment, even a person born without developed arms and legs, like Kyle Maynard, can participate—and excel—in sports. A significant factor in providing disabled children the opportunity to become involved in athletics is the support of family and coaches. If given a chance, these young people can prove their vast potential to themselves and to others.

At home I dreamt about being a professional athlete and playing on one of my favorite Atlanta sports teams. My dreams made me the star athlete who performed coolly under pressure; I'd imagine replacing John Smoltz as the clutch pitcher on the mound for the Atlanta Braves in the middle of their pennant race.

In my dreams, the only limitation was my imagination— the real world was different. I never thought the dream world, where I was the star, would be any different from the real world. In my mind's eye, the only difference was that now I'd be playing for real.

The more stories I heard about how much fun my friends were having, the more I wanted to play alongside them. My passion for sports and my drive to succeed were enough, I told myself—I would stop at nothing in my pursuit to be a normal fifth grade student and a great competitor.

More than anything else, I wanted to be the quarterback who dated the cutest cheerleader and became an icon among my peers. I was convinced that football was my avenue to reach out for those dreams.

My parents often had different emotions about my ambition to try new things. My father would dream alongside of me; my mother kept my feet on the ground. She told me to focus on the things I could do; my dad, like me, thought I could do more if I just worked hard enough.

My mom is as close to my heart as anyone else, but her fear of my disappointment has always clashed with my stubborn belief that I can do anything. No one wants to see their child's passions lead to emotional letdown. She tried to teach me to see the success in whatever I did, even when I failed. She is a great supporter, and I've always valued her advice, even when my enthusiasm for things like football meant that I didn't always follow it.

I couldn't have been more excited when I brought home a flyer from school about the upcoming football tryouts. The teacher who passed me the flyer—after I asked her for one— was surprised to see me so animated about it. She obviously didn't see me as a football player.

My mother couldn't help but feel a twinge of sadness when she saw the joy in my face, because she knew the likelihood of my making the team wasn't great. My dad was out of town at the time and he wasn't there to fan my dream. So my mother and I had a long conversation about my expectations and the possibility of failure.

She made it clear to me that the odds were I'd end up as a water boy for the team, on the sideline instead of the field. But she thought I'd have fun, make a lot of friends by being a part of the team, and make my own contribution to it. I agreed with everything she said, silently knowing that I ultimately wanted to be an important athlete on the team.

My mom is much more social and outgoing than I am or my father is. Rather than just show up, she called the coach to ask him if I could tryout. She made it clear that I was very different from other kids he had coached, but she never implied that I couldn't be a player. Neither my father nor I would have had the guts to call the coach in the first place, but my mother did it out of her love for me. And while telling the coach I was different, she never said I couldn't do what would be asked of me.

The next day, she took me to the tryouts. Football wasn't her favorite sport, but it didn't matter. Even then, I appreciated that very few mothers would have taken a disabled son to tryout for a football team full of able-bodied kids; she did it out of love for me, and I loved her for it.

We drove into the community's park for the first time and saw all of the football and baseball fields. The park was full of kids using the batting cages and basketball courts. My mom pushed me along in my wheelchair. When we got close to the field, I jumped out and ran to where the kids were gathered to try out for the football team. I was relieved to see a lot of my friends from school were at the tryouts to. I asked some of my friends about what I should expect. They told me about the drills, and I saw no reason why I couldn't excel at them. I was a kid, I was finally at the football tryouts, and it was time for me to do my thing.

The first drill was a timed forty yard dash down the field. I was a little nervous as the line kept moving and it was closer to my turn. When it was my turn at last, I stepped up to the starting line. The assistant coach asked me if I'd be able to do the drill, and I gave him a nod of confidence. When he gave me the signal to go, I sprinted off as hard as I could.

I was in a dead sprint in my bear-crawl stance, which means all four of my limbs were on the ground and I ran like an animal. Then suddenly, halfway through the first forty yard dash, I ran into a big problem. The baggy t-shirt I was wearing slipped up my back and started to come off fast once I picked up speed. My arms were tripped up—so I immediately bucked myself up on my back legs and waved my arms to pull the shirt down.

As fast as I shot up to fix the problem, I was back down to the sprint. Everyone watching was impressed at the fact that I had run so fast, and there was a lot of applause coming from the parents on the sideline. The head coach came up to me after the drill was finished and told me he was very eager to have me play on his team.

I was incredibly thrilled to have done so well and shown everyone, myself included, that I could be a part of an organized and talented football team. We finished the tryouts with a couple of drills to test our agility, and I performed well. Then the coach directed prospective players about how to register for the team.

At the registration I had the opportunity to have a closer conversation with the coach, whose name was Tom Schie. He told me that I was picked for his team because of the ability I showed to play the game, and not for any other reason than that. Coach Schie also told me that he had a good idea of what position I'd be playing, but that I had to wait until the first day of practice to find out what it was.

Of course, I really assumed that I'd be the quarterback, and I chose number eight for my jersey because it was the same number of one of my sports heroes, Troy Aikman [former Dallas Cowboys quarterback] I always loved Aikman's toughness under pressure and ability to play through pain.

Electrified for the season to start, I went home after the registration and patiently waited for the first practice.

I went to the store with my father, and we bought additional padding to help protect my arms and legs. Since I wasn't able to wear shoes and I walked around on my arms, it was very important to have some type of protective covering on my limbs.

My dad decided to sew the ends of arm pads together to protect the ends of my arms and legs. After I got my shoulder pads and helmet, I couldn't help but stare at the equipment pile for weeks, dreaming about the upcoming season.

The tryouts were in the beginning of the summer after fifth grade, but the season didn't actually start until after school began again in the fall. For once in my life, I couldn't wait for school to start. . . .

Initially, the coaches only gave me the opportunity to play when the team was winning by a lot and they could afford some mistakes. They didn't have full faith in my potential to do well when the game was on the line. But I was committed to proving them wrong.

When I had a chance to play, I made the most of it by doing everything I could to shut down the offense on the line of scrimmage. More times than not, I'd be able to play for four to five plays at a time. That usually gave the coaches on the opposing team the chance to run the ball at me to see if they could score a few easy yards.

I was relentless in my attack on our game days. The opposing coach would soon refuse to run the ball anywhere near me when he saw how intense I laid my helmet into his running back. There was no man that could pass me when I was focused and prepared to do damage and earn my position on the starting team.

Coach Schie saw my desire. He knew I wouldn't let him down by not giving my fullest effort every single play that I was in the game. As a consequence, he started giving me a lot more playing time.

He would put me in as a fresh lineman when the score was close or even if we were down by a few points. As his confidence grew in me, my confidence grew in myself. And that confidence helped make me a better and more versatile athlete because I could play with more intensity. I loved playing the game, I loved helping the team, and I loved having the chance to prove myself on every down.

There was one instance where a coach from an opposing team told my coach he was going to "take it easy on the little guy in the middle." Coach Schie went berserk and made it very clear that I was an athlete there to compete, not a mascot for the team or someone who wanted people to feel sorry for him.

Coach Schie used his conversation with the other team's coach as our pre-game pep talk. My friends and teammates all went nuts. I became a motivator for them, not just a token member of the football team.

Coach Schie gave me a lot of playing time in that game, and the opposing coach ran the ball right at me the very first play that I came in. He did it with his largest running back, purposefully to spite my coach.

I was determined not to allow him to embarrass my team or my coach. I crushed the running back with all of the strength that I had in me. He went stumbling back, and my teammates joined me to make the gang tackle.

The coach didn't run a single play in my direction for the remainder of the game.

I live to be tested under stressful situations and to pull through in the clutch, but this time I was also defending the respect of my coach and my teammates, and it was a great feeling to succeed.

On the football field, I never made excuses. I wanted to succeed for my father, to make him proud of my ability to play the game. I wanted to make tackles for all my friends and teammates who knew I would never let them down. I wanted to make plays for Coach Schie, who truly believed in my dedication and abilities. And I wanted to reward my mother's dedication to me—thanks to her realism, I felt even better when good things happened.

11

Childhood Sports Are Too Expensive

Dennis Fermoyle

Dennis Fermoyle, hockey coach and public school social studies teacher, wrote the book In the Trenches: A Teacher's Defense of Public Education *and maintains a Web log that espouses the importance of public schools.*

Child involvement in sports is a positive thing, but if taken too far it can turn into a negative thing. For example, some parents are investing larger and larger amounts of time and money so that their child will have the best equipment and the best training in order to turn into the best athlete. As a result, athletics is becoming too expensive for many working class families. Also, those parents who spend hundreds—even thousands—of dollars often put undue pressure on the coaches to give their child athletes special consideration. Children need support from their parents, but in the case of athletics, parents need to be careful not to pay too high a price.

Ever since I was a young boy, I have loved sports. Sports has remained a major part of my life since I became a teacher, because, until I retired from my hockey position in March, I've always been a coach. A couple of days ago [June 2006], I came upon this article that was run by the *New York Times*: "A New Competitive Sport: Grooming the Child Athlete." Maybe people who read this article would think that coaches love to see parents who will do anything for their kids' athletic careers, but here's one who definitely doesn't. I think that by loving sports so much, we are wrecking what should be a good thing.

The Problem of Inequality

One problem with this is that we are pricing a lot of people out of our sports. Hockey people are as guilty as anyone for the excesses in youth sports, and we are paying the price in many communities. Hockey used to be a sport for kids from working class families. The Minnesota State Hockey Tournament used to be dominated by towns like Eveleth and other iron range communities in northern Minnesota, but that is no longer the case. Unfortunately, the game is turning more and more into an activity for the upper-middle class only. Working class parents just can't afford the sport anymore in most communities. From reading this article in the *Times*, it looks like a lot of other sports might be on their way to doing the same thing.

The Problem of Overbearing Parents

Another problem is that we end up with parents who become more dedicated to their kids' sports than the kids are. For the past several years, I have worked at hockey schools in the summer, and I've always felt uncomfortable when I've walked out into the lobbies of the arenas I've worked in and watched some of the parents. Hockey parents, like parents of athletes in all sports, tend to have high hopes for their kids, and they certainly can't be faulted for that. But so many of them seem to think that if they can find the right hockey school, or if they buy the right pair of skates, and get the perfect equipment, that this will be the key to stardom, scholarships, and maybe even pro contracts for their children. There are few things I find more sickening than seeing hockey parents doting over their young future stars. I can say that because it was just a few short years ago that I was doing some serious dot-ing of my own. I've often said that temporary insanity is a pre-requisite for being a hockey parent, and I passed the test with flying colors.

All high school coaches have some problems with parents, and there is no better sport to illustrate why this is so than hockey. For starters, children often start playing before they are five-years-old. The parents spend huge sums of dollars on equipment, and they are expected to provide transportation to and from practices and games until the player is in high school. The number of games youth hockey teams play varies from place to place, but it may well be fifty or more. Many parents have to plan nearly every weekend in the winter around youth hockey games and tournaments, and it's not unusual for the hotel bills by the end of the season to be in the thousands of dollars. Then in the summer, they often plan their vacations in such a way that they can spend hundreds or thousands of dollars to send junior to the best hockey schools.

The Problem of Excessive Investments

The result is that by the time the youngster is in high school, the parents have made enormous investments in time, travel, emotion and money to their child's athletic career. We have very, very committed parents, and some of these committed parents are going to be very hard to please. There may be hell to pay if the coach doesn't put junior on the varsity as a sophomore, or if he simply doesn't play him enough. As any-one who coaches knows, what "playing him enough" means for some parents can be an impossible standard to achieve. Worse yet, sometimes junior isn't very good, or sometimes he just gets tired of the sport. Now it's the coach's job to put him on the junior varsity, or more fun yet, to cut him from the team. For some reason, the parents who have made all those investments in hopes of stardom, college scholarships, and pro contracts aren't very understanding when that happens.

The pressures on coaches these days are enormous. Not only do many parents expect the coach to feature their sons or daughters as the star players on the team, but they also expect that the coach should be able to produce a championship team. After all, with all that talent, how can they lose? It is a rare parent who is able to look objectively out onto the field, court, or arena and say to his neighbors, "You know, our kids just aren't that good."

Once again, the majority of parents of kids I've coached have been wonderful, and the only times I'd hear from them was when they thanked me for my efforts at the end of the year. The problem is that during the season, the more difficult parents make it hard to remember that those reasonable parents even exist. If a student getting a bad grade in an academic class can cause a parent to become unreasonable, you can multiply that unreasonableness by a factor of ten or more when it comes to sports. Parents who are unhappy with a teacher usually don't like him. Parents who are unhappy with a coach often view him with unmitigated hatred.

Don't get me wrong! Despite all this I still think being involved in sports and other extra-curricular activities is a wonderful thing. I also think it's wonderful when parents encourage and support their kids. But parents have to be very careful. The activities our kids are involved in need to be things that *they really want to do* rather than things *we really want them to do*. And today, that's a lot easier said than done.

12

Schools Worry About Child Athletes Using Steroids

C. W. Nevius

C. W. Nevius writes a column that appears regularly in the San Francisco Chronicle.

The intense media coverage and congressional hearings about the use of steroids by professional baseball players have caused high school administrators and coaches to consider the prevalence of performance-enhancing drugs among their own athletes. A 2005 study by the U.S. Centers for Disease Control and Prevention reported that 4.8 percent of U.S. high school students had used steroids without a doctor's prescription, and another federally funded research organization found that almost 40 percent of high school seniors said steroids were very easy to acquire. Concerned about the serious health problems attributed to steroid use, many high schools would like to implement drug testing; however, its high cost—as much as $200 per test—will prevent most schools from doing so.

Parents know that when their kids play high school sports, there is always a meeting at the start of the season where coaches and administrators bring parents together to discuss grade-point averages and eligibility, rules of conduct and unexcused absences.

But in the last couple of years in California, there's often a meeting for something else—steroids.

C.W. Nevius, "Impact of Steroids Felt Across High School Sports," *San Francisco Chronicle*, September 20, 2006, p. A–14. Republished with permission of San Francisco Chronicle, conveyed through Copyright Clearance Center, Inc.

Every high school athlete must sign a pledge that he or she will not use anabolic steroids. Every coach and volunteer must complete the American Sport Education Program course on steroids. And finally, in many schools, such as Archbishop Riordan in San Francisco, parents are required to attend a meeting to discuss the use and abuse of steroids.

That's right, steroids in high school.

Awareness of Steroid Use

The state's interscholastic athletic governing board last year [2005] began requiring California's estimated 700,000 high school athletes to sign the pledge in the wake of the BALCO [Bay Area Laboratory Cooperative] drug scandal centered in the Bay Area and congressional hearings over the use of performance-enhancing drugs in baseball.

"They can't play unless they come to the meeting," says Riordan athletic director Ron Isola, who has been at the school 34 years. "And no, we wouldn't have thought of doing this five years ago."

There are several ways of looking at this. Schools are taking a preventive approach to performance-enhancing drugs; and they are finally catching up with what has been going on for years.

"I get calls from parents, coaches and family doctors," says Dr. Steven Ungerleider, a Eugene, Ore., psychologist and steroids expert who wrote the book *Faust's Gold*, about the East German Olympic drug program. "In the last several years, we have seen a complete shift in the awareness level."

Rod Jones, a standout basketball player at Riordan who will be playing for the University of San Diego next year [2007], says he hasn't heard about any kids using steroids at his school, but when he attended basketball camps, there were always players who seemed bigger and more muscular than everyone else.

"There's always a man-child," Jones says. "He's built like he is 25 (years old). You're never 100 percent sure about those guys."

There isn't any question about what has increased awareness. Performance-enhancing drugs not only have been given intense media coverage, but we are hearing the names of the professional athletes who have been involved.

"I'm a very strong supporter of how the media has done a public service in this," Ungerleider says. "The media attention and the congressional hearings have raised the dialogue, and it is now starting to trickle down to the high schools and even the middle schools. That is one of the BALCO legacies."

The question is: Now that we're aware of it, what can be done?

Education About Steroid Use

The meetings with families are certainly one step. Dr. Robert Napoles, a physician who specializes in internal and sports medicine, spoke to some 900 attendees at the second annual Riordan event this summer. He used the book *Game of Shadows,* by *Chronicle* reporters Lance Williams and Mark Fainaru-Wada as a visual aid and resource for what he thinks is a growing problem.

"One of the things I did was type in 'steroids' in Google," Napoles says. "I got over 3 million hits to buy anabolic steroids. I think it just comes down to (the fact that) this is one of the other things parents have to worry about."

[N]early 40 percent of high school seniors said steroids were "fairly easy" or "very easy" to acquire.

Napoles wasn't so interested in lecturing the parents about the ethics of using drugs to build a bigger, stronger athlete. He was more concerned about the serious long-term health problems that can crop up—from liver disease to ripped tendons.

Education is a good step. But is it enough?

Prevalence of Steroid Use

This year, New Jersey became the first state to announce that it would begin testing high school students. School officials cited statistics from the state health department showing that steroid use among New Jersey high school students had increased from 3 percent in 1995 to about 5 percent in 2001.

More recent studies show the same trend. A 2005 survey of high school students across the country by the national Centers for Disease Control and Prevention reported that 4.8 percent had used steroids without a doctor's prescription.

Not that anyone needs a doctor. A 2005 study by Monitoring the Future, a federally funded research organization, found that nearly 40 percent of high school seniors said steroids were "fairly easy" or "very easy" to acquire.

So shouldn't we all be testing our high school athletes? It is a good idea in concept, but the implementation isn't so simple. For starters, in the 2000–01 school year, there were 7 million high school athletes across the nation. That number has almost certainly increased.

[T]his is dangerous stuff—long term.

"It is a very cost-prohibitive thing," says Don Collins, the San Francisco section commissioner for the California Interscholastic Federation. "Each test can cost as much as $200. It's not cheap."

New Jersey is hedging its bets, testing only randomly at postseason games. In fact, only about 500 of the 10,000 athletes who typically make state championships in 31 sports will be examined. And even at that, the cost is expected to be up to $100,000.

School districts, already strapped for cash, will have a tough time putting that kind of money together, especially in a state the size of California.

The sad fact is that unless money is somehow made available to schools, we can only warn parents and athletes of the risks—and hope for the best. Those who are abusing performance-enhancing drugs are clearly gaining an advantage in sports, but that's not really the issue.

"It's ethics, fair play and a level playing field," says Ungerleider. "But at the end of the day, the real message is, this is dangerous stuff—long term."

13

Parents Should Try to Make Sports Fun for Their Kids

Joel Fish with Susan Magee

Author and lecturer, Dr. Joel Fish has worked as a sports psychology consultant for U.S. Olympians, the Philadelphia Flyers hockey team, and the USA Women's National Soccer Team. Contributor Susan Magee is an award-winning writer whose work has appeared in The Philadelphia Inquirer Sunday Magazine *and* The North American Review.

Child athletics has become extremely organized, specialized, and competitive—so much so that many kids do not enjoy playing and are dropping out. While it is true that negative athletic experiences such as getting laughed at, teased, or ridiculed by teammates or coaches can create a lack of confidence and poor self-esteem in a child, the many positive and lifelong experiences—like goal setting, perseverance, teamwork, and physical fitness—make athletics a valuable contribution to a child's life. Parents are the deciding factor. When child athletes receive support and understanding from their parents, they will stay involved with sports and reap the many benefits for years to come.

As a licenced psychologist and sport psychologist with over 20 years of clinical experience dealing with a wide range of athletes, both professional and amateur, I have met and worked with many parents. In fact, I meet parents every day who tell me they feel confused, stressed out, or simply unsure of how to deal with the many issues and pressures raised by

Joel Fish and Susan Magee, *101 Ways to Be a Terrific Sports Parent*. New York: Simon & Schuster, 2003. Reproduced by permission of the publisher and the author.

their child playing a sport. These are hardworking, caring moms and dads from all backgrounds, walks of life, and income levels who have lots of questions—lots and lots of them—but few answers when it comes to helping their kids have a positive sports experience.

I routinely hear questions from concerned parents like:

My child seems quieter since joining the soccer team. Could he be stressed out?

My daughter's field hockey coach pushes very hard; is this okay?

Our son seems totally disinterested in sports. Should we sign him up anyway?

My daughter wants to quit the swim team mid-season. Will letting her quit send a bad message?

I'm a single mom raising a teenage son. He seems obsessed with winning. Is this just normal "boy" behavior?

Our eleven-year-old daughter is into skateboarding but we worry that there's an unhealthy subculture that goes with it. Is this true?

Sports Have Become More Organized

It's no wonder that some parents feel they have more questions than answers. Youth sports have changed quite a bit over the years, but especially in the last twenty years. Sports parents today often find themselves in uncharted territory.

When I was a kid (I'm 48 years old now [2003]), after school or during the summer, I just walked out the back door, grabbed a baseball or hockey stick, and headed out to the street or to a nearby field to find some other kids to play with. We played for hours with no uniforms, no refs, no parents on the sidelines urging us to victory. Sure, I liked to win;

we all did. But if we didn't it wasn't the end of the world. We thought, "We'll get them next time."

We played for hours. We played until the sky became so dark we couldn't see the ball anymore. We played until our mothers had to force us back inside. We played hard because we loved to play. It was fun.

Then, kids who played sports were just playing games, often with whoever was available from the neighborhood or playground. Now, kids who play sports are highly organized on teams and in leagues. Few kids are let out of the door and sent off to play or left to their own devices. There is far less spontaneous play.

Now, kids are coached, trained, conditioned, and judged. Most youth sports occur on teams or in leagues—there are fewer and fewer pickup games. Back when we were kids, if we played on a team, it was most likely a school team and we played for the school year and then we stopped. Now there are school teams that end but recreational leagues, after-school leagues, intramural sports, weekend leagues, summer leagues, sport camps, and year-round travel teams that go on and on.

Today, there are sports and competitions for things that weren't even considered sports when you were a kid—in-line skating, snowboarding, downhill racing, and skateboarding. The range of sports today is incredibly diverse.

[T]he most critical factor in whether the forty million sports-playing children love their sports experiences or hate them is the behavior . . . and the attitude of their parents.

I'm sure you don't need me to tell you that youth sports today are not like when you were a kid—you're living it. You're the one out there juggling schedules, shuttling your child to practices, attending the games and shelling out the money for uniforms and equipment.

Many Children Are Unhappy Playing Sports

In many ways, the changes that have occurred in youth sports since you were young are extremely positive. The sheer volume of kids playing sports today is terrific. It used to be that only the talented kids could play on teams; now kids of all skill levels can participate and that's good news for everybody. One of the reasons the number of sports-playing kids has skyrocketed is because the opportunities for girls to play sports has exploded in the last twenty-five years. In fact, one out of three sports-playing kids today is a girl. Kids can also participate now at younger ages. It used to be only school-aged kids had the chance to play organized sports. In general, kids of all ages, everywhere, have the opportunity to play more kinds of sports than ever before.

All great things. But there is a downside to all the changes in youth sports today.

Though a record forty million kids are playing sports, too many of them are unhappy. In fact, over 30 percent of them are quitting, dropping out, and throwing in the towel by the time they're thirteen!

The reason?

According to studies conducted by the Youth Sport Institute at Michigan State University, the majority of kids who quit sports say it's because they're not having any fun. Kids today feel too much pressure to win.

Think about that for a minute. That's nearly twelve million kids who were not having any fun playing soccer, basketball, hockey, tennis, and many other sports. Twelve million kids! That's a lot of kids who become disenchanted with sports. The sports-playing kids I work with often tell me they feel stressed out, worried, and overwhelmed. Something is very wrong. Sports is supposed to be fun! Once, not so long ago, it was fun.

In today's highly organized and specialized youth sports environment, more and more sports-playing kids feel that just giving their best during a game or competition is not good enough. At younger and younger ages, kids are sent the message: "If you don't win, don't play. Winning is the reason we play. Winning is everything."

When winning is everything, the competitive environment can become a stressful and negative place for youngsters.

When winning is everything, sports is no longer fun.

The high dropout rate in youth sports does not just hold short-term consequences for your child. The experiences we have as children playing sports help shape us as adults. For better or for worse, our early sports experience leaves its mark upon us. Athletics is one of the arenas in which, as children, we develop our identities. Self-esteem and self-confidence issues are frequently raised. A child with a poor athletic image and little confidence in sports may feel bad about him- or herself for years to come. The memories your child will have from the big game, the big race, the tournament, often stick to them like glue. Even events that happen at routine practices and games can profoundly influence your child for years to come, like getting laughed at or teased by teammates and how they are treated by coaches. I work with many adults, including professional athletes, and I can tell you that the memories we carry with us from sports are powerful ones. I know because adults frequently share their memories with me. Sports memories are typically vivid; the emotions attached to them are surprisingly fresh and often quite painful.

If your child is quitting sports, or is at risk to quit later, because she isn't having fun, whatever negative experience she has had may well follow her through adulthood. That's certainly not good. If your child drops out of sports, he won't reap the many benefits that sports has to offer—like goal setting, perseverance, teamwork, and fitness. That's not good either.

Sports Parents Can Make a Difference

Parents frequently ask me, "How can I make sure that my child has a good experience in sports? What's the secret?"

Some parents believe the secret is finding the right coach. Others say it's all in how she gets along with her teammates. Still others believe the secret is to match him with the sport that best fits his personality and temperament.

Yes, coaches, teammates, and the sport he plays matter. But the most critical factor in whether the forty million sports-playing children love their sports experiences or hate them is the behavior—both public and private—and the attitude of their parents. This fact surprises many parents.

Certainly, outside people and outside factors matter, and yes, these outside influences do contribute to shaping your child. But there's no doubt about it—parents always have had, and always will have, the most significant influence over their kids. What you think about your child is more important to him than what anyone else thinks. If your daughter feels, "Mom and Dad are proud of me," that is more significant than acceptance from a coach or peer. But if your child feels, or even gets a hint, that Mom and Dad love me more when I play well or when I win, then that puts her under a lot of pressure. Kids who feel too much pressure to win don't enjoy sports. These are the kids who either quit youth sports or wish they could. . . .

In sports, you cannot script the outcome of events. You can't always get what you want. We cannot guarantee that our sports-playing kids will have a good time or a good experience. We cannot guarantee that as parents we won't make some mistakes. But I can promise you this: If you are knowledgeable and aware of what your child is experiencing emotionally and physically in sports, you will be better able to give your child what he or she needs in order to have a good experience. When sports-playing kids get what they need from their parents—the right kind of love, support, guidance, and encouragement—they will stick with sports and reap many benefits for years to come. And when that happens, everyone wins.

14

Playing Sports Can Obscure Other Talents

Robin Gerber

Robin Gerber, a national commentator and speaker on leadership, is a senior fellow at the Robert H. Smith School of Business, University of Maryland, and a member of USA Today's *board of contributors.*

Many parents—often with good intentions—steer their children into playing sports. However, youth athletic programs have become so structured and specialized that kids are training and competing year round, which leaves little or no time to explore other interests and activities. In a July 2000 report, the American Academy of Pediatrics recommended that children be encouraged to branch out and diversify their talents. Experts in child development agree that instead of focusing on the high-stress field of athletics, parents should support their children in developing other aspects of their individuality.

My 13-year-old son Sam is a strong athlete. His talent has led to school years that he has channeled into a life of non-stop sports. But this summer [2003] at sleep-away camp, he had the time and opportunity to make a discovery. Sam sent an excited letter home that left my husband and me speechless.

Sam had landed the part of Peter Pan in the camp play. He learned 55 lines and three songs, spent hours in rehearsals all in pursuit of wearing a funny green hat and tights. What happened?

Like many kids, Sam's narrow casting in sports cheats him out of the chance to discover his more diverse talents and interests. In a well-rounded camp program that included everything from arts and crafts to physical activities, Sam had an opportunity that his laser-focused schedule at home doesn't allow: to try something new.

There Is More to Life than Sports

I've seen kids in my neighborhood groomed for sports as if their destiny had been handed down on a tablet at birth. But by zeroing in on what may be a child's early, and often fleeting, interest or by steering children based on preconceptions about what they should be doing, parents cancel out the rich experience of childhood discovery.

Fred Engh, CEO of the National Alliance for Youth Sports and author of *Why Johnny Hates Sports*, echoes that sentiment. He says a parent's job is "to help children discover anything about themselves and their talents. Some of the greatest artists will never be known because they were made to be basketball players."

Engh says part of the problem is the growth of sports-specialization programs. More young athletes are going to after-school and weekend training. Some parents are even hiring personal coaches. The results are kids who are training and competing year round.

Statistics show that specialization in sports is eating up more of our children's time.

I confess we paid for individual basketball instruction for Sam when his coach suggested his shot needed some work. Ironically, or perhaps by way of a lesson for parents, Sam says he has learned more playing pickup basketball at the local school with the older teens and men who show up most evenings. But kids have fewer and fewer chances for pickup games.

Playing Sports Monopolizes Children's Lives

Statistics show that specialization in sports is eating up more of our children's time. According to a study by the University of Michigan's Institute for Social Research, from 1981 through 1997 children's time in structured sports increased by more than 25% per week, while time spent in less-stressful activities such as youth groups and unstructured play each fell by roughly the same amount.

Kids as young as age 5 are in leagues. At the park in my neighborhood, I saw a soccer coach conducting a clinic for toddlers. And the impact for boys is double despite the increase in girls' sports activities brought about by Title IX. While the increase in structured time was equal for boys and girls, boys spent twice as much time overall as girls in sports.

Why the push and what's the hurry? Engh thinks parents are motivated by fear of their child not making a coveted team or dreams of creating the next Tiger Woods or getting college athletic scholarships. The intense actions of parents at children's sports events suggest kids' best interests may not be the key factor behind their grueling grooming. But does early specialization help these athletes achieve "Michael Jordan" dreams or hopes of a free ride in college?

Diversity Is Important in a Child's Development

Not according to the American Academy of Pediatrics. In a July 2000 report, the academy reports that research "supports the recommendation that child athletes avoid early sports specialization. Those who participate in a variety of sports and specialize only after reaching the age of puberty tend to be more consistent performers, have fewer injuries and adhere to sports play longer than those who specialize early."

All of the pressure may end up sending young athletes not into a stadium of cheering fans, but onto the psychiatrist's couch for feeling like a failure based on one thing: sports.

The academy goes on to recommend that children be encouraged to try different activities and learn diverse skills. Failure to give kids those opportunities can have psychological consequences, as well.

Jennifer Waldron, writing for the Institute for the Study of Youth Sports, cites some signs of the mental fatigue that too much athletics can cause. Children may have an "'I don't care' attitude, lowered self-esteem, feelings of depression and fear of competition."

Dan Gould, a professor in the Department of Exercise and Sport Science at the University of North Carolina at Greensboro, has written that chronic stress is caused by an athlete's perception that others see that person only in an athletic role, and by the lack of control the athlete feels in his or her life. If Waldron and Gould are right, all of the pressure may end up sending young athletes not into a stadium of cheering fans but onto the psychiatrist's couch for feeling like a failure based on one thing: sports.

One way to give kids a feeling of control is to encourage them to test new skills. That means parents have to let go of their own fantasies of what our kids should be.

Child psychiatrist Stanley Greenspan, author of *The Secure Child*, says, "From the time that our children are babies and we follow their lead in floor-time play to the ways in which we hang out with them and tune into their interests as school-age children, we are giving them the rarest of gifts—support for exploring a full range of interests and their pride in who they are and who they'll become."

No doubt Sam has a different view of himself now that he's saved Tinkerbell and defeated Captain Hook. And while I hope he'll still play soccer, I intend to have some fall brochures for pottery, cooking and dance classes on his bed when he gets home.

15

Child Athletes Should Keep Winning in Perspective

Arthur Riegel

Arthur Riegel is the father of eight children and has coached youth sports for twenty years. He is the founder of Enlightened Training Adventures, which espouses the motto "Play what you love and love what you play."

Many people have heard the statement "Winning isn't everything; it's the only thing," and attribute it to legendary Green Bay Packers football coach Vince Lombardi. But what Lombardi actually said was, "Winning isn't everything, but wanting to win is." It's an important distinction and one that every child athlete should understand. If kids think that winning is the only thing that matters, they will put too much pressure on themselves and feel like failures when they lose. Instead young people should play sports because they enjoy the game; winning is a bonus. Loving the game—whether it be the game of life or sports—is everything, and child athletes need to keep that in mind when they play.

This familiar quote idea has haunted me throughout all my years of coaching, and I suspect I am not alone. In case you are reading this and have no idea where this quote came from let me give you a little background. The saying "Winning isn't Everything . . . it's the Only thing" has for over 45 years been attributed to the legendary coach of the Green Bay Packer football team, the man for whom the Super Bowl trophy is named; the great Vince Lombardi. News flash: he never said it; what he did say is "winning isn't everything—but wanting to win is." The misquote comes from a Hollywood production starring John Wayne and Donna Reed, titled *Trouble Along the Way* (Warner Brothers 1953) that was filmed in black and white and was a story in which Wayne plays a coach and a single parent with a daughter at a private Catholic college and Donna Reed a social worker concerned about the child. In the film there is a scene in which a game is being played while Donna Reed and the little girl are up in the stands watching. The scene shifts between shots of the Duke [John Wayne] pacing along the sideline barking out plays and getting his team fired up, then to a couple of priests waving the school colors and finally to Donna Reed and the little girl who looks to be about 10–12 years old. Donna Reed is commenting to the girl about how she hopes the boys are enjoying the game and giving their all or something like that, when the little girl responds back with the line . . . "well you know what father (so and so) always says. . . . 'Winning isn't everything; it's the only thing.'" This is a line that came from a Hollywood production out of the mouth of a 10-year-old fictious character. Somehow this line got attributed to Vince Lombardi (some say due to his religious affiliation with the Catholic church) and he spent the rest of his life right down to his last days attempting to correct that mistake with sports commentators and writers.

Winning Is Not the Only Thing

I suspect like many others, that this kind of thinking, that winning is the *only* thing, has dominated many a coach and parent's way of looking at sports competition, and when we or our children or our school's team is not winning at every contest then there must be something wrong. Is it possible that something else is being gained that for the moment neither I the parent nor I the coach can grasp in my moment of temporary setback? It is the notion of winning all the time that is so ingrained in our society that we do all kinds of things including ignoring our higher sense of self to achieve it. At times we are willing to do "whatever it takes" even if it means not doing the right thing. Confused yet? Of course you are because unfortunately, once we remove the mind set that "winning is everything" we are forced to look someplace else for the real purpose of these competitions. In looking [for] the answer I have discovered [it] is not in my head. It lies truly in the heart with a capital H, and, I will come back to that in a minute.

It is not in the winning or losing but in the competing that the athlete/artist is able to demonstrate his level of mastery.

If you look at winning and losing as a whole the fact of the matter is that every time you step onto a field your chances are 50/50. This is a very simple truth, the world as we can perceive it, is made up of a set of opposites, hot vs. cold, up vs. down, win vs. lose etc. Everything in creation is a world of duality. In fact you cannot experience one without the other. Imagine living with only daylight? Or only darkness? One complements the other. Without sorrow [there] is no joy. Without an opponent we don't get to play the game. So how do we operate then in this world of duality? And where do we put our attention in order to succeed instead of fail[?] And more to the point, how do we participate in competitive sports? The answer lies in our higher sense of self. There is a greater part of us that knows how to take all this duality and see it for what it is and what it is not. We are far more than just winners or losers in this game! We are in fact, the creators of our own destinies. And depending on how we notice and observe the workings of our own thoughts and the feelings they create we can see the good in both the winning and the losing. We can experience both the good and the bad of winning and losing, and not forget our true selves. This is not a new concept, Eastern forms of competition have been teaching this for thousands of years; they even refer to their sports as "arts" as in martial arts. The goals of which are not to annihilate or destroy opponents but to honor, respect and love them. The realization being that without an opponent the artist doesn't have any way to demonstrate the skills he has mastered. The competition is based on both opponents demonstrating their best, giving 100% and enjoying the chance to compete. It is not in the winning or losing but in the competing that the athlete/artist is able to demonstrate his level of mastery. Vince Lombardi's correction of the famous misquote "Winning isn't everything—but wanting to win is" has a very subtle but powerful distinction from winning is the only thing. That distinction lies in the power of our attention and intention. Why participate in an activity unless you do it to the best of your ability? Our intention should always be to do our best to win or succeed, however if on any given day we do not have the outcome we would prefer we are not meant to take that personally. We give our best, learn from our mistakes and simply get better as we grow. I have a personal motto that goes like this: "Make it personal; don't take it personal." What I mean by that is I want to do things to the best of my ability, I want to personally make it my business to give all that I can, while at the same time, remembering that if I succeed or fail it is not a real reflection of who I truly am, it is just the result of the best of my efforts at that time.

Commitment Is Also Important

I can remember a number of times in my coaching career and my parenting careers, when my son and I both learned lessons during his days as a pee wee flag football player. One season, he was drafted onto a team that could not win a game. He would complain on our rides home and at one point told me he didn't want to play anymore. I understood his pain, having been there as a coach and player myself, but also knew that there would be some value in continuing and following through with what he had committed to doing. After much discussion and persuasion on my part, he agreed to finish the season and to simply give his best no matter what the score was in any given game. His team never did win a single game in the regular season, but lo and behold a small miracle did occur. When it came time for the playoffs, his team was able to be successful at the two most important games of the year. That's right; they won the semifinal and the championship games. I took the opportunity to point out to my son that had he quit, he would have missed out on being a champion. We also discussed how you never really know how things might turn out if you keep your commitments and your word and just give your best.

Earlier I mentioned a Hollywood movie that produced a very dangerous and unrealistic concept. Hollywood has also produced some very amazing and wonderful stories to inspire us as well. I recently watched "Friday Night Lights" another movie about football. It is all about the highly competitive game of Texas High School football. The best part was the scene in the locker room at half time of the "big game" when the coach starts talking about "Being Perfect", the team's context for the season. He starts off by telling the players to just forget about what's on the scoreboard, to forget about winning, and just go back out on the field to give their best, to give their all for each other and to do it with love in their hearts, and a sense of joy for playing the game. He tells them how much he loves each of them and he models for them what he hopes they have learned. . . . If they play the game to the best of their ability, and for all the right reasons, the final score is not their reward; the feeling they leave with will be. This is the real answer we are all looking for, the answer we find in our Heart with a capital H. In the game of football or the game of life, if we play full out, giving our best and loving what we do, there will only be winners and champions no matter what the scoreboard says. Playing the game for all the right reasons is the key.

Loving the Game Is What Matters

Finding and understanding the right reasons to compete was and is the biggest challenge I face on a daily basis no matter what the task. I live in this world of duality and by nature I have a preference for only half of what makes up my perception of reality. I only want to win, I only want happiness etc. The problem is the more attached I am to what I want, the more I also become attached to their opposites. Reality is a dual edged sword. The answer to this puzzle is in not being attached, but rather to play the game from your heart and not your head. You see, it is your head and your ego that sees and experiences the duality and it is your head that creates the preferences based on all the information it has collected over a lifetime of living in this world of opposites. It is your head that will take the winning and losing personally; your heart on the other hand will just go with the flow feeling the joy and love of simply playing the game. It is love that takes you back to the game—time and time again—whether you are winning or losing. In other words, Love isn't everything . . . it is the only thing. Winning is a happy byproduct.

Winning isn't everything—it's loving what you do that means everything.

A few years ago while I was as an assistant coach at the high school level; I was listening to our head coach talk to the players at halftime of a varsity basketball game. He told them that in order to be winners they would have to work hard, play smart, have fun and do it together. I found that to be very good advice. And as I was listening to him speak these ideas, it dawned on me that before anyone would ever want to commit to all the hard work it takes to win, something else would need to be present as well. The reason we become real winners and champions in sports and in life, is mainly that— aside from committing to the hard work, the playing smart, the fun, etc.—they had to truly love what they are doing.

If you love what you are doing it is far easier to put in the work, rebound from the losses and show up to play the game over and over again. As it turns out, when you examine the mindsets and hearts of true champions (whether in sports or in life) what you see and hear from them is how much they love it. Whatever the "it" is for them. All great champions have this as the basis for participating in their chosen endeavors. All great people have learned to play the game from their heart and simply use their head as a compass—a tool to navigate their way to success. This is the most valuable lesson, sports and competition has taught me. This is the most valuable lesson we can teach our young athletes. "Winning isn't everything—it's loving what you do that means everything."

Organizations to Contact

The editors have compiled the following list of organizations concerned with the issues debated in this book. The descriptions are derived from materials provided by the organizations. All have publications or information available for interested readers. The list was compiled on the date of publication of the present volume; the information provided here may change. Be aware that many organizations take several weeks or longer to respond to inquiries, so allow as much time as possible.

American College of Sports Medicine
401 W. Michigan Street, Indianapolis, IN   46202-3233
(317) 637-9200 • fax: (317) 634-7817
Web site: www.acsm.org

The largest sports medicine and exercise science organization in the world, ACSM promotes healthy lifestyles and is committed to the diagnosis, treatment, and prevention of sports-related injuries and to the advancement of the science of exercise. It publishes the newsmagazine *Sports Medicine Bulletin* and the quarterly *Fit Society Page*, which contains such articles as "Youth Sports & Health: The Right Time for Kids to Exercise" and "Working with Overzealous Parents in a Youth Sport Setting."

American Orthopaedic Society for Sports Medicine
6300 N. River Road, Suite 500, Rosemont, IL   60018
(847) 292-4900 • fax: (847) 292-4905
e-mail: aossm@aossm.org
Web site: www.sportsmed.org

Founded in 1972, AOSSM is a national organization of orthopaedic surgeons dedicated to sports medicine, research, and communication to ensure health and safety at all levels of sport. Among its many publications are the bimonthly newsletter *Sports Medicine Update* and the brochure *Youth in Sports.*

Athletes for a Better World
1740 Barnesdale Way NE, Atlanta, GA   30309
(404) 892-2328 • fax: (404) 892-2329
Web site: www.abw.org

The staff at ABW advocate a "Code for Living" that encourages discipline, integrity, respect, cooperation, and compassion in the sport environment. The organization provides free printed materials and a quarterly newsletter.

Boys and Girls Clubs of America
1275 Peachtree Street, NE, Atlanta, GA   30309-3506
(404) 487-5700
e-mail: info@bgca.org
Web site: www.bgca.org

BCGA's mission is to enable all young people to reach their full potential as productive, caring, responsible citizens. The organization offers a sports, fitness, and recreation program to youths with the goal of increasing their physical activity and to strengthen interactive relationships.

Center for Health and Health Care in Schools
2121 K Street, NW, Washington, DC   20036
(202) 466-3396 • fax: (202) 466-3467
e-mail: chhcs@gwu.edu
Web site: www.healthinschools.org

CHHCS, a nonpartisan policy and program resource center, was established to strengthen the well-being of youth through effective health programs and health care services in schools. It publishes the monthly e-journal *Health and Health Care in Schools* and the newsletter *Weekly Insider*.

Institute for Preventive Sports Medicine
P.O. Box 7032, Ann Arbor, MI   48107
(734) 572-4577 • fax: (734) 459-0814
e-mail: info@ipsm.org
Web site: www.ipsm.org

The institute researches ways to reduce sports-related injuries and disseminates research findings to benefit the public. IPSM provides numerous free publications and news releases.

Jeremy's Heroes
900 Route 9 North, 6th Floor, Woodbridge, NJ   07095
(877) 654-6773
e-mail: info@jeremysheroes.org
Web site: www.jeremysheroes.com

This nonprofit organization is dedicated to building character and confidence in America's youth through sports. It publishes the newsletter *Instant Replay*.

Kids Sports Network
8206 Roughrider, Suite 104, San Antonio, TX   78239-2449
(210) 654-4707 • fax: (210) 646-9977
e-mail: ksntexas@ksnusa.org
Web site: www.ksnusa.org

KSN is a nonprofit organization dedicated to promoting and enhancing youth sports through the education of coaches, parents, and administrators. It acts as a clearinghouse for youth sports information and conducts a variety of special events and programs. KSN publishes the quarterly newsletter *Time Out* and provides links to such articles as "Steroids: Just the Facts," "Preventing Injuries in Youth Sports," and "When Should Kids Start Sports?"

Let the Kids Play
P.O.Box 5073, Petaluma, CA   94955
(707) 695-9879 • fax: (425) 648-7325
e-mail: info@letthekidsplay.com
Web site: www.letthekidsplay.com

Let the Kids Play is a program for coaches and administrators to effectively manage the behavior of spectators in order to promote a positive environment for youth sports. The organization publishes the fact sheet "Let the Kids Play."

Moms Team

MomsTeam Media, Concord, MA   01742

(800) 474-5201

Web site: www.momsteam.com

MomsTeam is a comprehensive resource center providing parents the information and tools they need to manage their youth sports experience. It publishes a free newsletter as well as many articles including, "How to Balance Youth Sports with Family Life" and "Kids Just Wanna Have Fun."

National Alliance for Youth Sports

2050 Vista Parkway, West Palm Beach, FL   33411

(561) 684-1141 • fax: (561) 684-2546

e-mail: nays@nays.org

Web site: www.nays.org

The NAYS is a nonprofit organization that advocates for positive and safe sports and activities for children. It offers programs and services for everyone involved in youth sports experiences, including professional administrators, volunteer administrators, volunteer coaches, officials, parents, and young athletes. It publishes the magazine *Sporting Kid* and provides links to numerous informative articles and books.

National Council of Youth Sports

7185 S.E. Seagate Lane, Stuart, FL   34997

(772) 781-1452 • fax: (772) 781-7298

e-mail: youthsports@ncys.org

Web site: www.ncys.org

Through education and information, NCYS promotes the active participation by all youth in fun and healthy physical activities and encourages positive attributes such as fair play and good citizenship. Among its publications are the newsletter *Youth Sports Today* and the booklet *Win or Lose: A Guide to Sports Parenting*.

National Women's Health Information Center

8270 Willow Oaks Corporate Drive, Fairfax, VA   22031
(800) 994-9662
Web site: www.womenshealth.gov

The NWHIC, a service of the Office on Women's Health in the U.S. Department of Health and Human Services, works to improve the health and well-being of women and girls in the United States through programs, education, and dissemination of health information. The center provides the monthly newsletter *Healthy Women Today* and such publications as *Eating Disorders—BodyWise Handbook* and *A Lifetime of Good Health: Your Guide to Staying Healthy.*

Nicholas Institute of Sports Medicine and Athletic Trauma

130 East 77th Street, 10th Floor, New York, NY   10021
(212) 434-2700
e-mail: info@nismat.org
Web site: www.nismat.org

NISMAT is the first American hospital-based facility dedicated to the study of sports medicine. Its Web site offers information and links about nutrition, physical therapy, cardiology, training, orthopedics, and other hot topics. The institute also provides numerous publications and research reports.

Positive Coaching Alliance

3430 W. Bayshore Road, Suite 104, Palo Alto, CA   94303
(866) 725-0024 • fax: (650) 739-0270
e-mail: pca@positivecoach.org
Web site: www.positivecoach.org

Established at Stanford University in 1998, the nonprofit PCA provides live, research-based training workshops and practical tools for coaches, parents, and leaders involved with youth sports programs to teach life lessons through positive coaching. The alliance offers a video called *Honoring the Game: A Vision of a Positive Youth Sports Culture* and publishes written guidelines for coaches and parents as well as a monthly newsletter.

Team-Up for Youth
310 Eighth Street, Suite 300, Oakland, CA   94607
(510) 663-9200 • fax: (510) 663-1426
e-mail: info@teamupforyouth.org
Web site: www.teamupforyouth.org

Team-Up for Youth provides technical assistance, gives grants, and influences public policy to advance the field of youth sports, especially for girls and children in low-income neighborhoods. Among its publications are the newsletter *Ready, Set, Go!* and the fact sheets "Youth Sports Promote Youth and Community Health" and "Girls' Sports Facts."

Youth Enrichment Services
412 Massachusetts Avenue, Boston, MA   02118
(617) 267-5877 • fax: (617) 266-6168
e-mail: info@yeskids.org
Web site: www.yeskids.org

Youth Enrichment Services is a nonprofit organization that works with city youths to provide outdoor and environmental education programs. Among its publications are a biannual newsletter and the Harvard study "Impact Assessment: Youth Enrichment Services."

Bibliography

Books

Bob Bigelow, Tom Moroney, and Linda Hall	*Just Let the Kids Play: How to Stop Other Adults from Ruining Your Child's Fun and Success in Youth Sports*. Deerfield Beach, FL: Health Communications, 2001.
Joel Fish with Susan Magee	*101 Ways to Be a Terrific Sports Parent*. New York: Fireside, 2003.
Vincent M. Fortanasce	*Life Lessons from Little League: A Guide for Parents and Coaches*. Champaign, IL: Sports Publishing LLC, 2005.
David Galehouse and Ray Lauenstein	*The Making of a Student Athlete*. Sunnyvale, CA: Advisor Press, 2004.
James G. Garrick and Peter Radetsky	*Anybody's Sports Medicine Book: The Complete Guide to Quick Recovery from Injuries*. Berkeley, CA: Ten Speed Press, 2000.
John R. Gerdy	*Air Ball: American Education's Failed Experiment with Elite Athletics*. Jackson: University Press of Mississippi, 2006.
John R. Gerdy	*Sports: The All-American Addiction*. Jackson: University Press of Mississippi, 2002.

Jane Gottesman   *Game Face: What Does a Female Athlete Look Like?* Geoffrey Biddle, ed. New York: Random House, 2001.

Christine Grimes   *Student Athlete Handbook for the 21⁰ Century.* Lulu.com, 2006.

Ralph I. Lopez   *The Teen Health Book: A Parents' Guide to Adolescent Health and Well-Being.* New York: W. W. Norton, 2002.

Madeline Levine   *The Price of Privilege: How Parental Pressure and Material Advantage Are Creating a Generation of Disconnected and Unhappy Kids.* New York: HarperCollins, 2006.

Kyle Maynard   *No Excuses.* Washington, DC: Regnery Publications, 2005.

Michael A. Messner   *Taking the Field: Women, Men, and Sports.* Minneapolis: University of Minnesota Press, 2002.

Jordan D. Metzl and Carol Shookoff   *The Young Athlete.* Boston: Little, Brown, 2002.

Cal Ripken Jr. and Rick Wolff   *Parenting Young Athletes the Ripken Way: Ensuring the Best Experience for Your Kids in Any Sport.* New York: Gotham, 2006.

Jeff Rutstein   *The Steroid Deceit: A Body Worth Dying For?* Boston: Custom Fitness Publishing, 2006.

George Selleck · *Raising a Good Sport in an In-Your-Face World: Seven Steps to Building Character on the Field—and Off.* Chicago: Contemporary Books, 2003.

Harry Sheehy with Danny Peary · *Raising a Teen Player: Teaching Kids Lasting Values on the Field, on the Court, and on the Bench.* North Adams, MA: Storey Publishing, 2002.

Michael Silver and Natalie Coughlin · *Golden Girl: How Natalie Coughlin Fought Back, Challenged Conventional Wisdom, and Became America's Olympic Champion.* Emmaus, PA: Rodale Books, 2006.

Jake Steinfeld · *Get Strong: Body by Jake's Guide to Building Confidence, Muscles, and a Great Future for Teenage Guys.* New York: Simon & Schuster, 2002.

Bruce Svare · *Crisis on Our Playing Fields: What Everyone Should Know About Our Out of Control Sports Culture and What We Can Do to Change It.* Delmar, NY: Sports Reform Press, 2004.

Bruce Svare · *Reforming Sports before the Clock Runs Out: Man's Journey Through Our Runaway Sports Culture.* Delmar, NY: Sports Reform Press, 2004.

Periodicals

ABC News · "How to Handle 'Sidelines Sports Rage': Parents Behave Badly at Kids' Games," August 13, 2005.

Jennifer Alsever | "A New Competitive Sport: Grooming the Child Athlete," *New York Times*, June 25, 2006.

Amalie Benjamin | "When Play Is Work: Elite Aspirations Require Devotion of Young Athletes," *Boston Globe*, September 26, 2006.

Center for Health and Health Care in Schools | "Experts Cite Physical Activity as Key in Preventing Childhood Obesity," *Health and Health Care in Schools*, vol. 6, no. 9, December 2006. www.healthinschools.org.

Beverly Creamer | "Assault of Coach Rare, but Blatant," *Honolulu Advertiser*, October 25, 2006.

Matthew Davis | "Pressure Driving Young to Steroids," *BBC News*, May 3, 2005. http://news.bbc.co.uk.

Elizabeth Fitzsimons | "Challenge of Black Belt: The Rigors of Korean Martial Art Help Boy, 12, to Excel Despite Cerebral Palsy," *San Diego Union-Tribune*, October 28, 2006.

Robin Gerber | "Sports Craze Cuts Out Chance to Discover Other Talents," *USA Today*, August 4, 2003.

Susan Greenwald | "Victories by and for the Disabled," *U.S. Society & Values*, December 2003.

Kirk O. Hanson   "Culture Suggests Cheaters Do Prosper," *San Jose Mercury News*, March 6, 2005.

Health News Digest   "Amid Concerns of Obesity in Young People Doctors See Another Problem: Overdosing on Sports," *DentalPlans.com*, September 19, 2005. www.dentalplans.com.

Steven Horwitz   "Anabolic Steroids: Your Child's Road to the Gold or to the Grave?" *MomsTeam*, September 1, 2006. www.momsteam.org.

Guy LeMasurier and Charles B. Corbin   "Top 10 Reasons for Quality Physical Education," *Journal of Physical Education, Recreation & Dance*, August 2006.

Seth Livingstone   "Fight Against Steroids Gaining Muscle in High School Athletics," *USA Today*, June 8, 2005.

Howie Long   "Give Kids the Gift of Time," *Sports Illustrated*, October 16, 2006.

Mayo Clinic.com   "Keeping Kids Active: Ideas for Parents," *CNN.com*, January 26, 2005. www.cnn.com.

Mayo Clinic.com   "Performance-Enhancing Drugs and Your Teen Athlete," January 5, 2007. www.mayoclinic.com.

Mayo Clinic.com   "Strength Training: OK for Kids When Done Correctly," January 11, 2006. www.mayoclinic.com.

Terry Monahan   "Confronting Steroids: Ending the Silence," *North County Times*, September 19, 2005.

Shane Murphy   "The Cheers and Tears: Be a Parent, Not a Coach," *MomsTeam*, August 15, 2006. www.momsteam.org.

New York Times   "A Crisis? As Stakes Rise, More Parents Are Directing Rage at Coaches," June 28, 2005.

Josh Parks   "The Skinny on Weight Training and Steroid Use," *Parent Map*, July 2005. www.parentmap.com.

Ronnie Polanecsky   "A Gun at a Kids' Game? A Gun?" *Philadelphia Daily News*, October 24, 2006.

Marija Potkonjak   "Young Athletes Push Hard and Pay the Price with Injuries that Can Often Be Avoided," *East Valley/Scottsdale Tribune*, October 17, 2006.

Gilbert Quinonez   "Sports Fans, Parents Push Child Athletes Too Early," *Daily Bruin*, October 7, 2004. www.dailybruin.ucla.edu.

Eric Sondheimer   "Athlete's Mental Health Still Should Be Top Priority," *Los Angeles Times*, October 13, 2006.

Jacqueline Stenson   "Pushing Too Hard Too Young: Take Away the Fun Factor in Sports and Kids Can Burn Out," *MSNBC*, April 29, 2004. www.msnbc.com.

Kelly Wallace   "The Pressures of Kids' Sports: Competition Can Tax Time, Patience and Integrity," *cnn.com*, June 23, 2005. www.cnn.com.

Patrick Welsh   "Forum: Kids Losing Again: Ego-Driven Parents, Club Coaches Burning Children," *USA Today*, August 23, 2004.

Duff Wilson   "Steroids Are Blamed in Suicide of Young Athlete," *New York Times*, March 10, 2005.

Index